Perception

Paul Rookes and Jane Willson explain perception and perceptual processes in a way that almost anyone can understand. The study of perception, or how the brain processes information from the senses, has fascinated psychologists and philosophers for a long time. *Perception* takes the key research areas and presents the arguments and findings in a clear, concise form, enabling the reader to have a quick working knowledge of the area.

This clear and informative text discusses sensation and perception then looks at theories and explanations of perception. The way visual perception is structured is examined, followed by an analysis of the development of perceptual processes. The authors then consider individual social and cultural variations in perceptual organisation.

Perception will be particularly useful to students new to higher-level study. With its helpful textbook features to assist in examination and learning techniques, it should interest all introductory psychology students.

Paul Rookes has been teaching psychology for 25 years and is a senior examiner and moderator for A-level Psychology. He is also Team Leader for Psychology courses at South Trafford College, Cheshire.

Jane Willson has be   and has
considerable   Leader
for the AEB   College.

Routledge Modular Psychology

Series editors: Cara Flanagan is the Assessor for the Associated Examining Board (AEB) and an experienced A-level author. Kevin Silber is Senior Lecturer in Psychology at Staffordshire University. Both are A-level examiners in the UK.

The *Routledge Modular Psychology* series is a completely new approach to introductory level psychology, tailor-made to the new modular style of teaching. Each short book covers a topic in more detail than any large textbook can, allowing teacher and student to select material exactly to suit any particular course or project.

The books have been written especially for those students new to higher-level study, whether at school, college or university. They include specially designed features to help with technique, such as a model essay at an average level with an examiner's comments to show how extra marks can be gained. The authors are all examiners and teachers at the introductory level.

The *Routledge Modular Psychology* texts are all user-friendly and accessible and include the following features:

- practice essays with specialist commentary to show how to achieve a higher grade
- chapter summaries to assist with revision
- progress and review exercises
- glossary of key terms
- summaries of key research
- further reading to stimulate ongoing study and research
- website addresses for additional information
- cross-referencing to other books in the series

Also available in this series (titles listed by syllabus section):

Perception

Theory, development and organisation

Paul Rookes
and
Jane Willson

London and Philadelphia

First published 2000
by Routledge
11 New Fetter Lane, London EC4P 4EE

Simultaneously published in the USA and Canada
by Taylor & Francis Inc.,
325 Chestnut Street, Philadelphia, PA 19106

Routledge is an imprint of the Taylor & Francis Group

© 2000 Paul Rookes and Jane Willson

Typeset in Times by Keystroke, Jacaranda Lodge, Wolverhampton
Printed and bound in Great Britain by TJ International Ltd, Padstow, Cornwall

British Library Cataloguing in Publication Data
A catalogue record for this book is available from the British Library

Library of Congress Cataloging in Publication Data
Rookes, Paul, 1954–
Perception : theory, development, and organisation / Paul Rookes
and Jane Willson.
p.   cm. — (Routledge modular psychology)
Includes bibliographical references and index.
ISBN 0–415–19093–2 (hbk)—ISBN 0–415–19094–0 (pbk.)
1. Perception. I. Willson, Jane, 1950– II. Title. III. Series.
BF311.R635 2000
152.—dc21   99-057669

ISBN 0–415–19093–2 (hbk)
ISBN 0–415–19094–0 (pbk)

Contents

Illustrations

Figures

Tables

Acknowledgements

The series editors and Routledge acknowledge the expert help of Paul Humphreys, Examiner and Reviser for A-level psychology, in compiling the Study aids chapter of each book in the series.

They also acknowledge the Associated Examining Board (AEB) for granting permission to use their examination material. The AEB do not accept responsibility for the answers or examiner comment in the Study aids chapter of this book or any other book in the series.

The authors and publishers would like to thank all the copyright holders of material reproduced in this volume for granting permission to include it. Every effort has been made to contact authors and copyright holders, but if proper acknowledgement has not been made, the copyright holder should contact the publishers.

Introduction to perception

Introduction

As you read the text on this page, you are demonstrating your extraordinary powers of sensation and perception. You are able to identify letters and words at a remarkable speed and, if you glance up occasionally, you will be able to take in the sights and sounds and movements of objects and people in the room you are sitting in.

The aim of this chapter is to explain the nature of perception and to show why psychologists are interested in trying to explain perceptual processes. It will also give you an idea of how the visual system functions.

Sensation and perception

Sensation refers to the responses of sensory receptors and sense organs to environmental stimuli. **Perception**, on the other hand, is a process which involves the recognition and interpretation of stimuli which register on our senses. Someone who is studying sensory processes is likely to ask questions such as 'How is electromagnetic radiation registered by the eye?' Whereas a psychologist interested in perception is more likely to ask 'How can you recognise that object? How far away do you think it is? Where is it in relation to other objects that you see around you?' In other words, perception relates to how we make sense of our environment and sensation refers to the basic stimulation of the sense organs. Imagine that you hear someone play a few notes on the piano – the qualities such as pitch, tone and loudness register as sensations but, if you recognise that the notes form a tune, then you have experienced a perception. Most psychologists would agree that the boundary between sensation and perception is rather fuzzy. It can be difficult to decide just how complex stimuli need to be before they involve perception and how much interpretation is required before sensation becomes perception.

Why do psychologists study perception?

We usually use our senses with such ease that it may be difficult for you to understand that there is anything for psychologists to explain. Imagine that you are in a student common-room during a fairly quiet time. You will be able to recognise friends as they come in. You will be able to smell the coffee in their cups. You will be able to hear and understand the news headlines coming from a television set in the corner of the room. Perception just seems to happen – you do not appear to be expending much effort on it. Consider some situations where your quick perceptions can keep you from harm. They can alert you to a car that comes hurtling round a bend in time for you to jump back out of danger. They can provide you with information that makes you step back from an uncovered manhole in the pavement, so avoiding a fall and serious physical harm. The apparent immediacy of perception, however, belies the complex processes that are happening behind the scenes. There is an old saying 'Seeing is believing', but this is misleading. Look at the drawings in Figure 1.1. In spite of what your senses tell you, A, B and C are all perfect squares. Perception amounts to rather more than meets the eye!

Psychologists are interested in trying to understand some of the hidden complexities of perception. They ask questions such as:

- How are coherent perceptions derived from the myriad inputs being received all the time by sensory receptors?
- How are sensory data processed to provide mental representations of our environment?
- How important are factors like past experience in determining our perceptions?

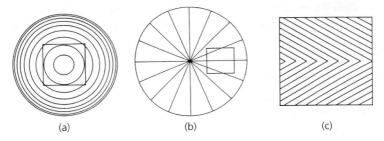

(a)   (b)   (c)

Figure 1.1 **Some examples of drawings that create misperceptions**

These questions will be addressed in later parts of the book, but you will find that psychologists do not all agree on the answers.

Explain briefly in about 50 words what is the essential difference between sensation and perception.

Progress exercise

The visual system

Perception involves *all* the senses but the theories that we will discuss in later chapters are concerned with visual perception. Vision is arguably the most important sense for humans and much more research has been conducted by psychologists into the area of visual perception than into any other perceptual systems.

In order to understand more about visual perception, it is worth knowing something about the way in which the visual system is constructed, although it is beyond the scope of this book to provide a highly detailed account. You will find excellent descriptions in more specialised textbooks (some suggestions are given at the end of this chapter).

Our sense organs are able to receive electromagnetic energy from the environment and to convert it into electrical activity in the nervous system. In vision, the environmental energy is in the form of light. We will trace the progress of the light signal through the visual system, noting along the way the various factors that can alter or impede the visual experience.

The structure of the eye

Incoming light from the visual stimulus needs to be brought into focus on the rear surface of the eyeball; it is at the **cornea** (see Figure 1.2) where this process starts.

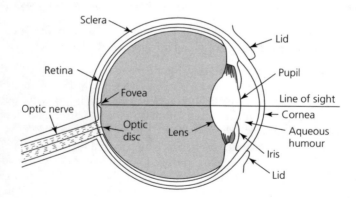

Figure 1.2 Diagram to show the structure of the eye

Cornea

The cornea helps to bend incoming light rays so that they fall directly on to the **retina** at the back of the eyeball. In some people the cornea is misshapen, causing an **astigmatism** which will give rise to blurred vision. Astigmatisms can be corrected using glasses but need to be detected early in childhood because they can otherwise lead to abnormal neural development. The cornea cannot be nourished by blood-vessels because they would block incoming light. Instead, it is provided with oxygen and nutrients by the aqueous humour – a watery liquid that fills the chamber immediately behind the cornea. This liquid is replenished continually but the canal through which this recycling occurs can become blocked, giving rise to a buildup of pressure called **glaucoma**. This can cause blindness if it is not detected quickly but can be easily treated.

The sclera which you perceive as the white of your eye is opaque and ensures that light can only enter via the cornea. However, you know from your own experience that you have to function under a wide range of lighting conditions and, when it is very bright, the cornea would let in far too much light for efficient vision.

Iris and pupil

The visual system deals with this problem by having a mechanism which controls the amount of light that can enter at any one time. This mechanism consists of a ring of coloured muscle called the iris. The pigmentation is important in restricting incoming light, and darker irises (e.g. dark brown) are usually more efficient than paler ones (e.g. light blue). In the middle of the iris is the pupil which is simply a hole through which light passes. The muscles of the iris are capable of constricting (i.e. making the pupil smaller) or of dilating (i.e. making the pupil bigger). When the light is bright, the pupil can contract to as little as 2 mm. in diameter but, in dim light, it can dilate to more than 8 mm.

You can demonstrate this easily with a friend or fellow student. Turn down the lights, leaving enough light so that you can see your friend's pupils. You will notice how large the pupils appear under these conditions. Shine the beam of a torch into your friend's eyes and see how the pupils constrict. Once the torch is turned off, the pupils will increase again. Note that this is a reflex action which is not under voluntary control.

Lens

This is a spherical body located immediately behind the pupil. Its function is to complete the task begun by the cornea of bringing light waves into focus on the rear of the eyeball. The curvature of the lens determines the degree to which light is bent and, by changing its shape (a process called **accommodation**), it can focus light rays from both near and distant objects. The newborn human infant cannot accommodate and is only able to focus clearly at a distance of approximately 19 cm. (i.e. the approximate distance of the baby's face from the mother during feeding). Images of objects at other distances are blurred. The ability to accommodate develops fairly quickly during the first couple of months of life. However, as we grow older, the lens loses its elasticity and it becomes more difficult to focus on close objects. This is a condition called **presbyopia** and is common in people aged over about 50 years. However, it can be corrected by wearing glasses. It is also worth noting that the lens is not completely transparent. It is tinted yellow and the density of this tint increases with age. The yellow pigment screens out some of the blue and ultraviolet light entering the eye and, as it becomes denser with age, can alter our colour perception. Sometimes, as a result of injury, disease or old age, the lens can become cloudy and this can become dense enough to cause blindness. Clouding of the lens is called a **cataract** and can be corrected by surgery.

Retina

The retina is a layer of light receptors (**photoreceptors**) and nerve cells at the rear of the eye. It is here that the transduction of light into neural energy takes place. It is only the thickness of a sheet of paper and yet it contains millions of cells arranged in layers. The retina contains two kinds of photoreceptors (**rods** and **cones**) and a variety of nerve cells (see Figure 1.3).

Fovea

Look back at Figure 1.2 and find the part of the retina called the **fovea**. This is a tiny area less than the size of the full stop at the end of this sentence, but it is the part of the retina that produces the clearest vision and is densely packed with cone cells. If you look directly at a target, your eyes are aligned so that the image of the target falls on the foveal region. Think about what you are doing while you are reading this page. You probably feel that all the words are clear and in focus. However, this is because, while you read, your eyes move repeatedly to register new words on your fovea. Try focusing on the F in the middle of the line below and, without

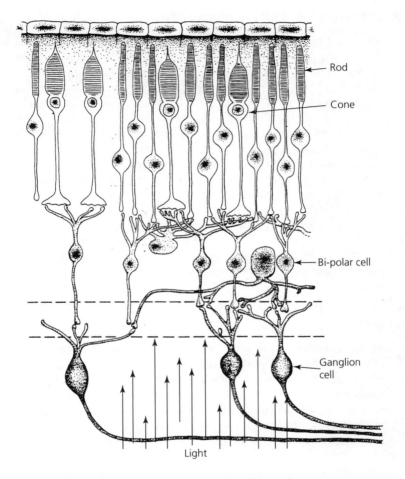

Figure 1.3 **Diagram to show a cross-section of the retina**

moving your eyes (don't cheat!), see how many letters you can see clearly on each side.

D X P A W N G B L F Z I Q H M S J V K

You probably found that your range was only about 3 letters either side and that any letters further away were blurred.

Rods and cones

The two types of photoreceptors have different functions. Cones provide our perception in daylight conditions and allow us to see in colour. Rods enable us to see under dim conditions although they allow only black and white perception. At night you will not see an image that falls directly on to your fovea because it contains only cones. You can test this for yourself. On the next reasonably clear night, go out into the garden (or any place where there are no bright lights nearby) and look up into the sky. Try and locate a dim star slightly to the left or right of where your gaze is directed. Shift your focus so that you are now staring at this star. You will find that it seems to disappear because it is now falling on your fovea where there are no rods.

The photoreceptor cells convert light into neural information which is then transmitted via the **bi-polar cells** to the **ganglion cells** and out of the eye into the brain. The way in which the photo-receptors carry out the conversion is complex and beyond the scope of this text.

Optic nerve

The **optic nerve** (see Figure 1.2) is a bundle of **axons** (the long fibres of nerve cells) which push through the back of the retina and carry information to the brain. There are no photoreceptors at the point where the optic nerve leaves the retina (**the optic disc**, see Figure 1.2) and so we are unable to respond to any light that falls on to this spot. The optic disc creates a **blind spot**. We are normally unaware of this in our everyday lives because constant movement and perceptual 'filling in' (see below) compensate for this 'black hole', but you can easily become aware of the blind spot by doing the following demonstration.

Look at Figure 1.4. Hold the page out at arm's length. Close your left eye and focus your right eye on the X. Keep your right eye on the

Figure 1.4 **Illustration to show the blind spot**

X and move the page slowly towards you. At some point, you will find that the square seems to vanish. This is the point where the image of the square is falling on your blind spot. This exercise also tells you something important about perception. Did you notice that, when the square disappeared, the line seemed to carry on continuously where the square should be? This shows that we seem to fill in the missing information automatically so that we do not experience holes in the visual field.

The optic nerves from both eyes come together at a point that looks like an X (the **optic chiasm**) (see Figure 1.5).

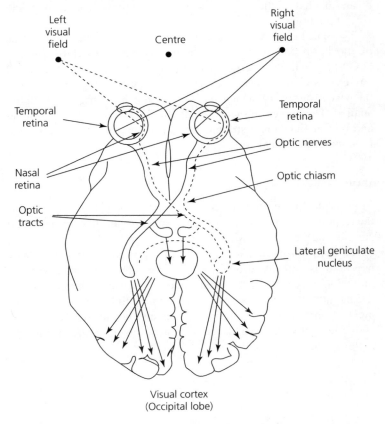

Figure 1.5 **Diagram to show the visual pathways from the eye to the visual cortex**

The nerve fibres from each eye are divided to represent the half of the retina closest to the nose (nasal retina) and the half of the retina closest to the side of the head (temporal retina). The fibres from the nasal retina cross to the opposite brain hemisphere at the optic chiasm while those from the temporal retina continue in the same hemisphere. This means that each half of the visual field will be projected to the opposite side of the brain. Look again at Figure 1.5 to make sure that you understand this. A common mistake is to think that each eye projects to the opposite side of the brain. However, the crossing over of half the fibres in each optic nerve in the optic chiasm means that half of the visual field of *each* eye projects to the opposite side of the brain.

The optic nerves (now called the optic tracts) continue on either side of the brain and travel through the **lateral geniculate nucleus (LGN)** to finally converge on an area of the brain called the **visual cortex** or **striate cortex**. There are more than 100 million neurons in the visual cortex of which only a fraction have been thoroughly studied. The pioneering work in this field was carried out by Hubel and Wiesel, but there is still much to understand about the nature and function of the visual cortex.

Summary

In this chapter we have differentiated between sensation, which is the response of sensory receptors and sense organs to environmental stimuli, and perception, which involves recognition and interpretation of sensory information. We also considered some of the reasons why psychologists are interested in studying perception. We concentrated on vision, since this is the most important sense for human beings and has attracted the most research. Incoming light from the environment is processed by various mechanisms in the eye before it is converted into electrical activity which travels along the neural pathways to the visual cortex.

One simple explanation of how the visual system works is that we operate like a camera. The eye has an aperture (pupil) which can vary its diameter to let in more or less light. It has a lens which can change its shape to focus on objects at different distances. Light reflected from the objects in the visual scene in front of us is focused by the lens on to the retina (the 'film' at the back of the eye). This forms an image which, just like in a camera, is upside-down and back to front. The image is then transmitted to a part of the brain where it is further processed to produce a mental representation of the scene (the finished photo). This can be a useful analogy but it is far too simple. Try to write down some of the differences between the human visual system and a camera.

Further reading

Carlson, N.R. (1998) *Physiology of Behaviour*, 6th edn, Boston: Allyn and Bacon. An up-to-date general text on physiological psychology which is well written and comprehensive. It is aimed mainly at undergraduates but the relevant sections on vision are fairly easy to understand.

Green, S. (1995) *Principles of Biopsychology*, Hove: Lawrence Erlbaum Associates. A very clear, easy to understand text suitable for A-level students. It contains concise chapters on sensory systems and vision.

Pinel, J.P.J. (1990) *Biopsychology*, Boston: Allyn and Bacon. Again, an advanced textbook but it is extremely clear and well written. It contains some excellent illustrations and has good chapters on the visual system and the mechanisms of perception.

2

Theories and explanations of perception

Introduction

In this chapter we will examine key theories of perception. Two important approaches to the problem of perception come from almost opposite directions. For example, some psychologists feel that perception is direct (e.g. Gibson) and all the information needed is contained in the visual display. Others believe that the brain uses past experience and other influences to construct a version of reality (e.g. Gregory).

Other theorists (e.g. Neisser) have attempted to reconcile these opposing views, and yet others have taken an **artificial intelligence** approach using knowledge about computer programs to help explain perceptual processes (e.g. Marr's computational theory).

The central question which needs to be addressed is: How do we perceive the world around us so quickly and generally so accurately? Researchers have taken two main approaches to this question and they can be broadly divided into two categories:

- **Bottom-up theories**
- **Top-down theories**

Top-down and bottom-up processing

Top-down and bottom-up approaches have been applied to virtually every aspect of cognition including perception. The terms are used to refer to the different methods of interpreting sensory data and they come from the **information processing approach** to the study of areas like memory, attention, perception, etc. This approach constructs models of the mind that are similar to the flow charts used by computer programs, and it sees the human brain as a machine which manipulates information through a series of processing stages.

Bottom-up processing

This is processing which begins with an analysis of sensory inputs. It is based on properties of the stimulus such as the distribution of light and dark areas or the arrangement of lines and edges in the visual scene.

The information which is acquired from these sensory inputs is then transformed and combined until we have formed a perception. The information is transmitted upwards from the bottom level (the sensory input) to the higher, more cognitive levels. This kind of processing is also called 'data-driven processing' because the information (i.e. the data) received by the sensory receptors determines (drives) perception.

So, according to this idea, we observe an object (e.g. a chair) and the visual system extracts simple, low-level features like vertical and horizontal lines. These simple features are then combined into more complex, complete shapes like legs, seat and back, and we finally perceive a set of integrated shapes which we recognise as a chair.

Top-down processing

Top-down processing is the reverse of bottom-up and is used to describe the higher, more cognitive influences on perception. It is based on the idea that sensory information from the retina is insufficient to explain how we interpret visual information. We also need to use our stored knowledge about the world in order to make sense of the visual input. This higher-level information works downwards from the top in order to influence the way in which we interpret sensory inputs. This kind of processing is also called 'concept-driven processing' because prior knowledge (stored mental concepts) comes from the top to determine (drive) interpretation of sensory input at the bottom.

Consider the following example:

Gregory claims that perception is a dynamic, constructive process

You should have no difficulty in reading this sentence as 'Gregory claims that perception is a dynamic, constructive process'. However, look carefully at the writing again. You will see that the 'cl' at the beginning of 'claims' and the 'd' at the beginning of 'dynamic' are identical, i.e. the image that falls on your retina will be exactly the same in both cases. Similarly, the 'n' in 'constructive' is the same as the 'u' in 'constructive'. The reason that you perceived them differently is that you read them within a context and that context influenced your interpretation of the written script. This is an example of top-down processing.

Now that we have explained the differences between bottom-up and top-down processing, you may be asking how it is that we can recognise a chair without reference to stored knowledge. Surely we only understand the concept of a chair because of our experience of seeing chairs in the past and our experience of sitting on them. All theorists, including bottom-up, acknowledge that there has to be some matching process between sensory information and stored mental representation in order for final identification (naming) to take place. We can only know the word 'chair' because it is stored in memory. The difference is that data-driven theorists assume that the matching process itself operates in a bottom-up direction until a match is found. The concept-driven theorists, on the other hand, assume that stored knowledge is required throughout the matching process. In other words, the question is whether our visual system can recognise a chair solely from a bottom-up analysis of individual features like four legs, differentiating it from other objects with four legs (e.g. a table, a dog, etc.), or whether our knowledge and experience with chairs in terms of factors, such as where they are likely to be found and the different shapes they can be, helps us in a top-down direction to recognise the object.

In practice, there is often an overlap between bottom-up and top-down processing. No single theory that takes an extreme view on the use of the two processing approaches can explain *all* the evidence we have from perceptual studies. It seems likely that we use both top-down and bottom-up processing in our everyday life. Whether we use one approach more than the other would seem to depend on the viewing conditions. We will discuss this in more detail when we look at individual theories.

Matlin and Foley (1992) have suggested that there are three reasons why our perceptions are a reasonably accurate mirror of the real world.

- Stimuli are rich in information.
- Human sensory systems are effective in gathering information.
- Concepts help shape our perceptions.

Palmer (1975) carried out a study to investigate the interaction of top-down and bottom-up strategies. He showed participants various drawings which they were asked to identify (see Figure 2.1). The sketchy line drawings in Figure 2.1(a) are very difficult to identify out of context. However, when they are put into the context of a face (Figure 2.1(b)), even though the drawing is quite unlifelike, the squiggles are easily identifiable as facial features. In recognising Figure 2.1(b) we are using both bottom-up and top-down processing. We recognise the face as a whole because we recognise the parts, but we would not be able to recognise the parts without the context of the whole. In Figure 2.1(c) we are able to recognise the features out of context (i.e using bottom-up processing) because they are rich in detail.

Gibson's theory of direct perception

Description

James Gibson maintained that perception is a direct process. He firmly believed that there is enough rich sensory information in the patterns of light reaching the eyes – he called this the **optic array**

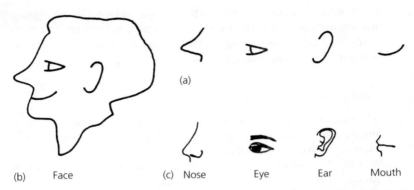

Figure 2.1 **Some of the drawings used by Palmer (taken from Palmer, 1975)**

– for recognition to take place without recourse to higher cognitive processes. This places his theory very firmly in the bottom-up camp. He was critical of the methods used by top-down theorists such as Gregory because he felt that they were artificial and ambiguous. Gibson was much more interested in perception as it occurs in the natural environment and, for this reason, his theory is sometimes known as an **ecological theory**.

Gibson's theory is quite complex and was formulated over a period of more than 30 years. We will focus here on the key aspects of the theory. Goldstein (1999) has suggested that there are four main principles:

- The proper way to describe a stimulus is not in terms of the retinal image but in terms of the optic array.
- The important information for perception is created by the movement of the observer.
- The key element of the optic array is invariant information (i.e. information that remains constant as the observer moves).
- It is the invariant information which leads directly to perception.

The optic array

Gibson felt that the starting point for perception should be the optic array (the structure or pattern of the light in the environment). An observer perceives objects, surfaces and textures in the visual environment because of the way the light rays reaching him or her are structured by the objects. This light structure is extremely complex because of the myriad rays that are converging on the observer from all parts of the scene.

The importance of movement

The real importance of the optic array for Gibson was not so much the structure at any one time but in how the structure changes as the observer moves. He called this the *ambient* optic array, which can be described as follows. Imagine you are sitting down at one side of a room facing a window. There is a low table between you and the window. Outside the window is a tree. When you stand up the optic array changes. The standing observer now has some new information about the environment; for example, he or she can now see behind the table and can see the tree from a new angle.

'Ambient' means 'surrounding', so Gibson was describing how most of our perception occurs as we move relative to our environment. Even if we are sitting down, we still move our heads to look around us. Gibson was interested in the information contained in the ambient optic array. He believed that a basic property of this information is that it is invariant, i.e. it remains constant even when the observer changes position or moves through the environment.

Invariant information from the environment

There are several sources of invariant information identified by Gibson. We will mention three of them:

- **texture gradient**
- **flow pattern**
- **horizon ratio**

Texture gradient occurs when a textured piece of ground like a pebbled beach or a grassy field is viewed from an angle. The individual elements (e.g. the pebbles or the blades of grass) are seen as being packed closer and closer together as the distance increases. Gibson called this invariant information because, as you walk across the beach or field, texture gradient continues to provide information about depth and distance – the further elements continue to look more densely packed. Consider an everyday example. Have you ever planned a picnic and looked out for a smooth area of grass? You start at the edge of the field and walk towards an appealing spot, only to find as you approach it that the grass is just as rough as it was at the edge of the field. It looks better further on however, so you trudge on, only to find that your new target is just as bad. This is an example of texture gradient making you see distant patches of grass as smoother and more densely packed.

A flow pattern

This is created as elements in the environment flow past a moving observer. If you look out of a train window as it travels through the countryside, you experience the rapid passing of objects like houses close to the railway line but the much slower movement of trees further away in the distance. This is an example of **motion parallax** which is a **depth cue** (discussed in Chapter 3), but Gibson emphasised the flow of the whole visual field rather than the relative movement of isolated objects.

Gibson investigated **optic flow patterns** (OFPs) particularly in the context of pilots' experiences in taking off and landing. When a pilot is approaching a landing strip, the point towards which he is aiming appears to remain motionless while the rest of the visual environment appears to move away from that point. These OFPs serve to provide pilots with clear, unambiguous information about their direction, speed and altitude.

Horizon ratio

This is the proportion of an object that is above the horizon divided by the proportion below. The horizon ratio principle states that when two objects of the same size are standing on a flat surface, their horizon ratio will be the same.

In Figure 2.2 all the telegraph poles have the same horizon ratio so we know that they are the same size. The tree, on the other hand, has a horizon ratio that is larger than the telegraph pole, so we know that the tree is taller than the telegraph pole. The horizon ratio is invariant so, even though the image of the telegraph pole itself may become

Figure 2.2 **An example of the horizon ratio**

larger on the retina as the observer moves towards it, the proportion of the pole that is above and below the horizon remains constant.

Direct perception

According to Gibson, this invariant information in the environment leads directly to perception.

Gibson seems to be able to account for our ability to locate objects spatially within the visual context but you may be wondering how he accounts for our ability to attach meaning to what we see. How do we realise, for example, that the object we are looking at is a chair and that we use it for sitting on? Gibson's answer is that visual perception does not occur in a vacuum and that we always find ourselves in a rich context which includes our:

- physical situation (e.g. in a classroom, on a train, etc.)
- psychological state (e.g. pleased, sad, angry, etc.)
- physiological state (e.g. highly aroused, thirsty, tired, etc.)

When we combine our physical and psychological states with our constantly changing optic arrays, we are enabled to recognise not only what the object is but what it does. Gibson called this the **affordance** of the object; for example, a cup affords drinking and a chair affords sitting down. The affordance chosen by the observer will depend on the factors mentioned above. Someone who is thirsty will perceive the affordance of a glass as for drinking. Someone who has just been given a bunch of flowers might see the affordance of the glass as a container/vase.

Evaluation

Visual perception is a very fast and accurate process. As soon as you open your eyes, the environment is perceived instantly. Studies where information is presented for brief periods of time indicate that some time is needed for processing but the processing (although variable) is measured in milliseconds. Direct perceptual processes would, by their very nature, be fast and accurate and this is the case. There would also be evolutionary pressure for perceptual systems to develop fast response times, as slow responses would make individuals more prone to predation.

Gibson himself paid little attention to physiological mechanisms but recent studies lend some support to Gibson's ideas. For example, it has been shown, at least in primates, that there are neurons in the **extrastriate cortex** which respond only to complex stimuli such as faces (Bruce *et al.*, 1981). There are also neurons which learn from visual experience to perceive specific forms (Logothetis and Pauls, 1995) and others which allow us to perceive properties of the environment as remaining constant even when we move about or view stimuli under different lighting conditions (Tovee *et al.*, 1994). It seems, then, that the physiologists may be discovering neurons which account for some of the direct perceptions which Gibson described.

Lee and Lishman (1975) conducted a study in which they used a specially built swaying room. They found that adults who were placed in the room usually made slight unconscious adjustments in order to avoid falling over. This kind of study tends to support Gibson's belief in the importance of movement in perception.

However, there are problems with his theory. The idea that meaning can be perceived directly (affordance) is one of the weaker

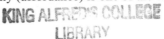

aspects of the theory. Human beings function in a cultural environment where knowledge of the use of objects is learned. Indeed, knowledge of the use of many objects is directly taught and would not necessarily appear simply by affordance. Bruce and Green (1990) have suggested that Gibson's concept of affordance may explain the visually guided behaviour of insects which have no need for a conceptual representation of their environment, but that is inadequate for explaining human perception.

Another problem for direct perception theories is the existence of visual illusions. Illusions demonstrate that the visual system can be inaccurate. Inaccuracies should not arise if perception is direct and relies on invariant and unambiguous properties of the optical array. Gibson believed that experiments using illusions were carried out in very artificial situations which had no relationship to the real world.

A clear demonstration that people tend to interpret situations from previous knowledge is provided by the Ames room (Figure 2.3). People view the person as being smaller and taller rather than being closer or further away. This is because rooms are usually box-shaped with right-angles. If the situation is arranged as in the Ames room the illusion works because of our assumption about room shapes and the fact that the room looks normal. This is significant because it shows that past experience and assumptions influence perception.

Gibson answered this criticism by asserting that our perception of the size of the two people in the room is based on how they fill the distance between the top and bottom edges of the room. Since one figure fills the entire space and the other takes up only a small part of it, we perceive the first figure as taller.

However, his explanations of how we experience perceptual illusions is not altogether convincing and does not account for all the experimental evidence in this area. His failure to account for the fact that we do not always perceive the world accurately remains one of the major weaknesses of his theory.

Constructivist theories

Background

The **constructivist** approach began over a hundred years ago with Helmholtz (1821–94), who believed that perception was based on a

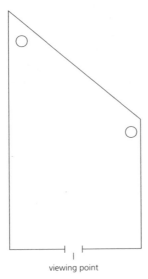

viewing point

Figure 2.3 The Ames room. Photograph reproduced with permission
from Eastern Counties Newspapers Limited

process of inference. He argued that, on the basis of the sensations we receive, we draw conclusions about the nature of the object or event that the sensations are most likely to represent. Because we make these inferences so quickly and without apparent awareness, he described the process as unconscious.

Modern constructivists suggest that the stimuli we receive from the environment are frequently ambiguous and have no clear-cut interpretation. This means that the observer has to solve the problem (or construct the best guess) as to the identity of the stimulus. In other words, the observer has to use indirect, top-down processes to make sense of the sensory input. Think back again to the example given on p.15, of

Gregory claims that perception is a clynamic, constructive process

You read that sentence easily and without any conscious awareness of solving a problem. You read the 'd' in dynamic as a 'd', even though exactly the same sensory input had just been interpreted a fraction of a second before as a 'cl' when it occurred in the word 'claims'. The only explanation for this would seem to be that you were processing an ambiguous stimulus input (handwriting) and having to find the most likely interpretation. 'Clynamic' is not a word whereas 'dynamic' is not only a proper English word but one that makes sense in the context of this particular sentence.

Some critics of the constructivist approach have suggested that such problem solving cannot take place without conscious awareness. However, this is completely untrue. Computers can carry out extremely complex mathematical problem solving that requires logical processing and yet machines have no consciousness.

Although the top-down processing involved in perception is believed to be largely unconscious and instantaneous, perception is seen to be *indirect* because information has to be processed at a level beyond the sensory level in order to be recognised accurately.

There are certain assumptions that all modern constructivist theorists share. Eysenck and Keane (1995) have suggested three shared assumptions:

1. Perception is an active and constructive process involving more than the direct registration of sensations.

2. Perception occurs indirectly as the end-product of the interaction between the stimulus input and the internal hypotheses, expectations and knowledge of the observer. Motivational and emotional factors can also play a part in this perceptual processing.
3. Perception is influenced by individual factors and this means that errors will sometimes be made, leading to inaccurate perceptions.

Gregory's theory

Gregory acknowledged the importance of Gibson's work in the area of perception, particularly with regard to his ideas about texture gradient and motion parallax. However, he could not accept Gibson's overall conclusion that perception occurs directly with no intervening higher cognitive processing.

Gregory wrote in his book *Eye and Brain* (1990, p. 219):

> The sense organs receive patterns of energy, but we seldom see merely patterns: we see objects. A pattern is a relatively meaningless arrangement of marks, but objects have a host of characteristics beyond their sensory features. They have pasts and futures; they change and influence each other, and have hidden aspects which emerge under different conditions.

Gregory believed that the information supplied to the sensory organs is frequently impoverished and lacks sufficiently rich detail for perception to take place. Instead, it is used as the basis for making best guesses about the nature of the external stimuli. For Gregory, perception involves a dynamic search for the best interpretation of the available data – a process he called hypothesis testing. A study conducted by Pomerantz and Lockhead (1991) supports the idea that top-down processes can influence perception. They briefly showed participants visual stimuli which they then asked them to identify.

Participants who were shown a single stimulus like the one in Figure 2.4(a) usually reported having seen a circle. However, when shown the two circles in Figure 2.4(b), they were much more likely to see the breaks as significant and to report that they looked more like the letters 'c' and 'u' respectively. This is an interesting finding and is probably best explained in terms of hypothesis testing or best guessing. When just one circle is presented, observers 'see' it as

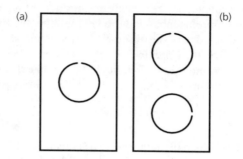

Figure 2.4 **Examples of stimuli similar to those used by Pomerantz and Lockhead (1991)**

a circle because they are used to seeing circles drawn by hand that are unintentionally imperfectly executed. However, when two circles are presented, both with an identical break but one which occurs in different positions, observers are more likely to conclude that the breaks, far from being unintentional, are highly significant and that they serve to distinguish between the two circles. When asked to describe the stimuli after presentation, participants seem to exaggerate the breaks (i.e. the circles become a 'c' and a 'u') because their hypothesis has led them to see the two circles as quite different from one another.

Gregory believed that individuals do not need much sensory data in order to formulate hypotheses. In a fairly recent article (1996), he cited a study by Johannson (1975) that seemed to support this idea. Johannson placed between ten and twelve small lights at points on a model's body (shoulders, elbows, knees, hips, wrists and ankles) and filmed the person moving around a darkened room. Participants viewing the film could make nothing of the apparently meaningless pattern of the lights if the model stayed still, but were instantly able to identify a 'walking person' once the model started to move.

Gregory himself was particularly interested in perceptual errors and made extensive use of visual illusions in his research. We will look at visual illusions in more detail in Chapter 3, but we need to consider them briefly here in order to understand Gregory's views.

Look carefully at the drawing called the Necker Cube in Figure 2.5. Concentrate hard on the drawing and try not to let your eyes stray. You will probably find that the cube suddenly seems to jump and presents itself in a new orientation. It might take you a while to experience this but, once it has happened, you will find that the cube continues to jump backwards and forwards between the two orientations. Gregory explained this by saying that the drawing is ambiguous. At first sight, most people test the hypothesis that the drawing represents a cube resting on a flat surface (e.g. a table). However, there is no surrounding context in the picture (i.e. no table is drawn), and so it is suddenly possible to see an alternative inter-pretation of the line drawing, namely that it is a cube mounted on a wall that is coming out towards the viewer. In the absence of either a wall or a table, however, the picture offers no clue as to which of the interpretations is most plausible so the viewer switches between the two. Gregory believed that, in the kind of viewing conditions that exist in everyday life, there will normally be enough contextual information to remove any ambiguity and to lead to the confirmation of a single hypothesis.

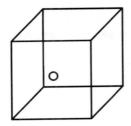

Figure 2.5 **The Necker Cube**

Gregory used other visual illusions to illustrate how we go beyond the information given in order to form perceptions; these will be discussed in Chapter 3. You will need to read the relevant section in that chapter in order to have a full understanding of Gregory's contribution to constructivist theory.

Perceptual set

Allport (1955), another constructivist theorist, introduced the concept of **perceptual set**. His thesis was that perceptual bias affects attention. Predispositions in the perceptual system make some stimuli stand out more from the background information arriving from the senses. So, for example, if you are particularly interested in cars, you are more likely to notice makes and models than someone who sees cars merely as a means of travelling from A to B. This theory is directly relevant to Gregory's constructivist ideas because it views perception as an active process involving information processing and interpretation.

Sets have a wide range of functions. They are affected by motivation, emotion, past experience and expectations and serve to make perception more efficient. This is achieved because sets reduce the choice between alternatives. This means that predisposition towards a stimulus will make any choice quicker than considering all the alternatives. Coren *et al.* (1987) demonstrated this by presenting an image like the one in Figure 2.6.

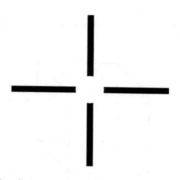

Figure 2.6 A stimulus figure similar to the one used by Coren *et al.* (1987)

Take a look at this yourself and see if you can detect a shape in the middle of the configuration of lines. Coren *et al.* found that, if participants were told in advance that they might see a circle, they tended to report back that a circle had been seen. If, on the other hand, they were told that they might see a square, they tended to report either that they had seen a square or no figure at all. Participants who were given no indication of what they were likely to see tended to report having seen either a circle or no figure at all. This seems to show that the circle is the dominant percept and that a square is only likely to be seen if a mental **set** can be induced first.

Expectancy can serve as a short cut to the interpretation of stimuli and aids planning and effective functioning in the environment.

Set has been found to be involved with many psychological variables such as motivation, emotion, context and beliefs. The effect of factors such as these on perception will be discussed in more detail in Chapter 5.

Evaluation

There are some problems with a very strong constructivist theory of perception. One clear hurdle is why people tend to see the world in a similar way if every person constructs their own perceptual model.

A further problem is that most people see the world correctly most of the time. Gibson believed that laboratory studies of perception were highly artificial and that illusions did not occur in the real world. This is not entirely so since illusions do occur in the real world, but not as frequently as Gregory's theory would predict, i.e. we are not easily misled. Many studies in this area involve presenting information that is fragmented and ambiguous, which means that people will use prior knowledge to try and understand what they are seeing because they have little else to go on. Presentations are typically also brief which reduces the scope for bottom-up processing. These factors suggest that constructivist explanations are magnified by the experimental situation and may be much reduced with normal rich environmental stimulation.

Gregory, unlike Gibson, has been quite successful in explaining why people experience perceptual illusions. However, his explanations cannot account for the fact that we continue to perceive an illusion such as the Müller-Lyer, even when we know it is an illusion. The Müller-Lyer (discussed in Chapter 3) is a drawing of two parallel straight lines, one with fins at each end pointing outwards and one with fins at each end pointing inwards (see Figure 3.7(a)). The straight lines are equal in length, but viewers experience the powerful illusion of one line being longer than the other. Even when viewers are given a ruler to check that the lengths are identical, they persist in the impression that the lines look different. This is difficult to explain and implies that the hypothesis is incapable of being modified in the light of experience. There is a related problem in that the hypothesis is supposed to be the best guess. Consider the Ames room (Figure 2.3). This is a specially constructed room which gives the illusion of having a normal, square construction but which has, in fact, a sloping rear wall. To an observer looking into the room, two people placed at either corner of the far wall will look very different in size. This poses a puzzle for the observer, who believes (wrongly) that the two people are the same distance away. Ittelson (1952) arranged for the two people in the room to walk along the back wall and pass each other. Because one of the two people is actually moving away from the observer and the other one is moving towards her, the observer will experience the retinal image of one person getting smaller and the other getting larger. This retinal size information usually gives information about distance but, in this case, the observer believes that the people are at the same distance from her. A bizarre and unlikely hypothesis for explaining this problem is to say that the two individuals are changing in size. A much more sensible hypothesis is to guess that there is something strange about the construction of the room. Surprisingly, very few observers draw the more appropriate conclusion.

Synthesis theory

Background

There are some similarities between the direct and constructivist positions. They both acknowledge, for example, that:

- Visual perception depends on light reflected from stimuli in the environment.
- Perception cannot occur in the absence of a physiological system to support it.
- Perception is an active process even though the two theoretical positions see the activity involved rather differently. For constructivists like Gregory, this is embodied in the notion of the perceiver as a hypothesis tester. For Gibson, the perceiver acts as a map-reader rather than a passive camera.
- Perception can be influenced by learning.

However, there are also differences and a central disagreement, as we have seen, is about the relative contributions of bottom-up and top-down processes. This may, however, be largely a reflection of the different experimental methods used by the two types of theorist.

Gibson tended to work in natural situations where viewing conditions were optimal. In these conditions, bottom-up processing probably has more impact. Gregory, on the other hand, used mainly impoverished or ambiguous visual stimuli where there is little scope for pure bottom-up processing. It seems likely, therefore, that in most circumstances a combination of the two is probably needed.

Neisser's analysis-by-synthesis model

Neisser (1976) tried to reconcile the direct and constructivist positions by proposing a cyclic model of perception. He acknowledged that we are more likely to recognise objects quickly if they appear in a situational context. Human perceivers, according to Neisser, start out with certain expectations about the kinds of things they are likely to encounter in a given context. Perception, according to this view, is not a linear, one-way process with an input that leads progressively to a single interpretation. Neisser sees it instead as an active, cyclic process in which the viewer has to check and re-check input against expectations. Figure 2.7 shows a schematic representation of Neisser's model.

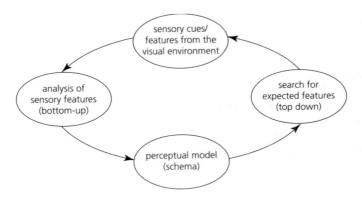

Figure 2.7 **Neisser's model**

Neisser believed that perception involves a series of processes.

Preliminary sampling   There are pre-attentive processes (i.e. they occur automatically and unconsciously) which produce a preliminary represen-tation of sensory data. This is bottom-up processing.

Direction

If the preliminary stage indicates some important stimulus, then attention is directed at it. The observer now uses schemata (packages of stored information about previous experiences) to help build a perceptual model (a mental representation of likely objects or events). This is top-down processing. The observer then compares this with the preliminary representation created at the first stage. This is called the inter-mediate representation and is the product of the interaction of bottom-up and top-down processing.

Modification

If the comparison with sensory data produces a match with the perceptual model, then this model can be accepted as the final perception. However, if the correspondence between the perceptual model and the sensory data is not perfect, the perceptual model will have to be revised until a perfect match is found.

Neisser called his model an analysis-by-synthesis theory of percep-tion. The synthesis involves generating a perceptual model based on past knowledge and experience which helps form perceptions in a top-down direction. The analysis involves analysing sensory data in order to extract relevant information about elements in the environment and this is passed up the system in a bottom-up direction.

Evaluation

There is no doubt that Neisser's theory is intuitively appealing. It combines perceptual hypotheses made on the basis of prior know-ledge or schemas with the extraction of sensory cues from the environment. The perceptual process is seen as a continuous active interaction between top-down and bottom-up processing and this seems highly likely.

However, there are some problems with the theory. A broad criticism is that the theory is too vague and does not specify exactly how schemas interact with the sensory data. It describes what we do but not how or why we do it. It is not clear exactly where and at what point the perception actually occurs in the cyclic process. Imagine that you go into your garden and see a black shape under a bush. Past experience gives rise to the perceptual model that this is your dog and you search for further dog-like features such as big paws and tail (bottom-up processing). However, you find no such dog-like features so have to abandon your first perceptual model and generate a new one. Perhaps it could be a black rubbish sack that has blown under the bush so you look for features such as the string tied round the top and the shiny surface of the plastic. You find these features and so your second perceptual model is confirmed. The question arises, though: At what point does a 'perception' emerge? Do you actually experience the shape in the first instance as your dog and then change your mind to see it as a sack, or do you only see the sack when the perceptual model is finally confirmed? And what if the black shape is neither of these two things but turns out to be a turkey that has escaped from a farm further down the road? You have never experienced a turkey in your garden before and so you are unlikely to have generated this perceptual model. Neisser does not explain how we experience totally unexpected perceptions.

Another criticism is that there is insufficient reference to the biological processes that might underlie the cyclic process of inter-actions between perceptual models and sensory data.

Computational theory

Background

The computational approach is a branch of artificial intelligence (AI) which involves designing computer systems to carry out cognitive tasks. Some researchers in this field design computers which can carry out perceptual tasks in a practical situation (e.g. computers that can detect faulty cells in a blood sample). Others develop computer programs which simulate mental processing in human beings. We will look at a computational theory that has attempted to establish a set of rules and procedures which govern vision. Theorists working in this area see visual perception as a problem and their aim is to provide a solution to the problem. They do this by providing a theoretical analysis of the solution and by describing the algorithms (problem-solving procedures) which work out the solution. AI researchers usually then run a computer program that mimics these algorithms. If the program actually works, it demonstrates empirically that this is a feasible explanation of human visual processing. Note that it does not necessarily *prove* that it is the correct way but only that it is a possibility. Marr, whose work made an important contribution to the computational approach, did not test out all of his proposals in this way and so some of them remain theoretical proposals.

Marr's model of visual perception

If you think back to Neisser's theory, you will recall that it can be criticised for failing to specify the processes which underlie the interactions between sensory input and stored knowledge. Marr (1982) argued that a comprehensive theory of visual perception should include at least three levels of explanation. These are:

- *The computational level.* This specifies the job that the visual system must do, i.e. its function.
- *The algorithmic level.* This is concerned with the detailed processes involved in perception.
- *The hardware level.* This is concerned with the neuronal mechanisms underlying perceptual processing operations.

Marr's approach is largely bottom-up, although there is some room for top-down processing in the later stages of perceptual processing. However, this aspect of his theory is less well defined than his description of the earlier stages of processing. The computational approach acknowledges the role of knowledge in perception but it is of a more general nature than the specific knowledge that the constructivist approach sees as necessary. General and basic knowledge about the laws of physics and geometry is used to analyse a complex scene into separate objects and shapes. Marr believed that the visual system carries out various mathematical computations about intensity changes in the image but, at the same time, takes into account what Marr calls the natural constraints in the world (basic properties of the environment). The computational approach is complex and highly technical and it is beyond the scope of this book to describe it in detail. We will present a summary of the main elements of the theory.

Marr believed that object recognition was a central feature of vision and he concentrated on this aspect of perception. According to his theory, perception begins with the retinal image and then proceeds via a series of stages. At each stage, the image is transformed into a more complex representation of the input. Marr described each stage in terms of the basic elements (or primitives) characteristic of that stage.

There are four main stages:

Grey level description	The intensity of light is measured at each point in the image.
The primal sketech	This is the result of the initial stage of computations but we do not see it at this stage. Before conscious perception can occur, we have to process the information contained in the primal sketch. We group together primitives of similar size and shape at this stage to form structures and outline shapes.
2.5-D sketch	At this stage, a 'picture' of the world begins to emerge. It is no longer a straight image because it now contains additional information. It provides depth cues such as shading, texture gradient and motion. It describes only the current visible surfaces of the scene (excluding unseen surfaces such as those hidden behind other objects) and will change if the scene is viewed from a different angle. For this reason, it is called viewpoint-dependent.
3-D model representation	At this stage, the viewpoint-dependent descriptions are converted into object-

centred description. The three-dimensional shapes of objects and their spatial interrelationships are perceived. Objects that are obscured from view will be represented in the three-dimensional model (e.g. the hidden leg of a chair). At this stage, prior knowledge may influence perception (e.g. you have to know that a chair is likely to have a fourth leg even if it is not currently visible).

Evaluation

Marr's theory has been very important in stimulating theoretical and empirical research. A fairly fundamental question is whether Marr's model works. Marr and Hildreth (1980) developed a program which analysed images successfully to the raw primal sketch stage. However, the fact that the program works does not necessarily mean that human perceptual systems operate in the same way.

There is some support for the model from neurophysiological studies, but further algorithms have been generated by other computational theorists which appear to correspond more closely to results from human perceptual experiments (see e.g. Watt and Morgan, 1984).

Marr stressed the importance of providing a complete explanation at three levels. However, if you think about the function of visual perception (computational level) it is not clear-cut. There are several functions (e.g. balance, navigation, object recognition, etc.) and they may all require a separate computational model. Marr concentrated principally on object recognition.

Much of the detailed work that Marr carried out was focused on the bottom-up strategies associated with the early stages of processing. In other words, he was most concerned with the processing steps before object recognition actually occurs. When he described the final stage where top-down processes are thought to occur, his ideas become much more sketchy and unconvincing.

Summary

In this chapter, we have looked at various theories of perception and distinguished between bottom-up and top-down processing. Gibson's theory rests on the assumption that perception is a direct process. He believed that we can extract sufficient information from the sensory stimulus to experience accurate perception. His theory accounts for some of the available data and has some support from neurological studies, but it cannot explain our experience of visual illusions.

Constructivist theories place more emphasis on the role of learning and experience, and advocates of this approach, such as Gregory, suggest that perception is akin to hypothesis testing. Such theories can account for our interpretation of ambiguous stimuli but have been criticised for artificial experimental techniques. Neisser attempted to provide a reconciliation between the direct and constructivist positions with his synthesis theory. This theory is quite attractive but is descriptive rather than explanatory. A more detailed model is the computational theory put forward by Marr. This theory has been very important in advancing our understanding of object recognition, but it is limited. All the theories discussed have strengths and weaknesses but there is, as yet, no single theory to account for all that is known about human perception.

Draw up a table listing the main strengths and weaknesses of the theories covered in this chapter.

Review exercise

Further Reading

Eysenck, M.W. (1993) *Principles of Cognitive Psychology*, Hove: Lawrence Erlbaum Associates. A straightforward account of perception which gives a solid base for further reading.

Eysenck, M.W. and Keane, M.T. (1995) *Cognitive Psychology: A Student's Handbook (3rd edn)*, Hove: Lawrence Erlbaum

Associates. Aimed at undergraduates and very detailed but also readable and user friendly.

Groome, D. (1999) *An Introduction to Cognitive Psychology: Processes and Disorders*, Hove: Psychology Press. Although aimed at undergraduates the text is clear and accessible with informative illustrations. Theories of perception are particularly well done.

3

Perceptual organisation

Introduction

It seems, as we have seen in earlier chapters, that perception is a much greater achievement than it at first appears. Even quite sophisticated computers which can beat world class chess players cannot yet be designed to match the visual capacities of even relatively primitive animals.

We are constantly presented with a diverse and ever changing array of sensory information and, as we move around, the patterns of light falling on the retina shift and change as well. In spite of this, we seem to be able to achieve a remarkably stable representation of our visual world. This suggests that our perception is highly organised and, in this chapter, we are going to look at some of the ways in which we organise our perceptions.

The question of how all aspects of perception came to be organised was central to a group of psychologists who formed the

Gestalt School of Psychology. They developed a set of principles to account for perceptual experience and these principles could legitimately be regarded as a *theory* of perception. We include them in this chapter, however, because the ideas relate so closely to perceptual organisation.

One factor that has intrigued psychologists is our ability to maintain stable perceptions even though our retinal image is constantly changing. People do not seem to shrink as they walk away from us and a clock on the wall continues to appear round even if the image falling on the retina is of an ellipse. Look around you now. The walls, table and window edges all appear to be rectangular, and yet the right-angles you perceive in the corners of the room or on the tables nearly all form acute or oblique angles on the retina. If you look through the window, cars passing by seem to be a normal size but they occupy much less space in the retinal image than your wristwatch. We see objects as the same size, shape and colour (i.e. as **perceptual constancies**), despite the fact that these objects can throw very different images on the retina depending on their distance and orientation.

We seem to 'construct' the world from our visual input rather than 'see' it directly. One remarkable fact about perception is that we are able to convert the two-dimensional sensation of the scene on our retina into the three-dimensional experience of perception. This seems to depend on using certain *cues* which give us information about depth and distance.

Human perception is usually accurate, but the perceptual system can sometimes break down, as a number of well-known **visual illusions** can demonstrate. Any adequate theory of perception needs to be able to account for both the failures of the perceptual system and the successes, i.e. why accurate (or **veridical**) **perception** is usually possible, given the apparently impoverished nature of some of the information available in the retinal image.

Finally, the complex issues of pattern perception and the perception of movement will be discussed.

Gestalt psychology

Most of the visual patterns we perceive are composed of a number of separate elements. These are not seen as a random, chaotic array of different hues and brightness levels but are instead organised into objects and groupings. We usually have no difficulty in seeing the boundaries of objects and separating out figures from their backgrounds.

The question of how we organise visual input into recognisable shape and form was a central concern for a group of psychologists (e.g. Wertheimer, Koffka and Kohler) who formed the Gestalt School of Psychology ('Gestalt' is a German word meaning 'shape' or 'form').They were interested in investigating how we are able to see whole objects standing out distinctively from their surroundings. They called this the **figure–ground relationship**. This refers to the organisational 'decision' that our perceptual system has to make, i.e. 'What is the thing being looked at and what is the background?'

Look at the shapes in Figure 3.1 and consider how you would describe them. Can you see any kind of pattern in them or do they simply look like funny, irregular shapes? If we tell you that the word 'fly' is contained in the spaces between the shapes, you will probably see it straight away. You are now able to impose some meaningful organisation on the shapes. Normally, we experience no difficulty in recognising words because the letters that make them up stand out as the 'figure' against the 'ground' of the white page. Because the familiar figure–ground relationship has been reversed in the above example, it is initially difficult to make sense of it.

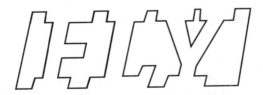

Figure 3.1 **An example of the figure–ground relationship**

The Gestaltists studied the properties of figure and ground by considering reversible pictures like the one called the 'Rubin Vase' shown in Figure 3.2. You will probably see quite easily that the picture can be interpreted as either a white vase on a black background or two black silhouettes of human faces looking at one another with a white screen behind them.

Figure 3.2 **The Rubin Vase**

The Gestaltists described several properties of figure and ground:

- The figure is more 'object-like' and more noticeable than the ground.
- The ground seems to be unformed material which extends beyond the figure.
- The figure is perceived as being in front of the ground.
- The edge (contour) separating the figure from the ground appears to belong to the figure.

It is almost impossible to see the faces and the vase at the same time and, as Baylis and Driver (1995) have pointed out, this reflects our experiences from real life. They posed the question: 'How likely is it that, in real life, a vase and two faces would have exactly the same contours?' The answer is that it would be possible but not very likely. It is even more unlikely that you would happen to be viewing them from such an angle that the contours coincided exactly (as in Figure 3.2). Baylis and Driver believe that the visual system is tuned to regularities in our environment and so it takes this unlikelihood into account. Therefore, when it perceives an edge dividing one object from another, it assigns that dividing edge to only *one* of the objects

– that object is then perceived as figure and the other as ground. This explains why we cannot see the vase and the two faces simultaneously in Figure 3.2. In real life, of course, we do not see many examples of ambiguous figure–ground relationships except in the case of camouflage. The colouring of some animals can protect them from predators or conceal them from intended prey by making them blend into their background. Regan and Beverley (1984), in a study of camouflaged figures in a laboratory, found that the figures could only be distinguished from the ground when they moved.

The Gestaltists also proposed a set of principles of perceptual organisation which described the way in which we group together elements to form a perceptual whole. They stated a law of organisation which encompassed all their other principles of grouping. This is called the **Law of Prägnanz** (law of good form) and was explained by Koffka in 1935 as follows: 'Of several geometrically possible organisations, that one will actually occur which possesses the best, simplest and most stable shape.'

This may be a rather difficult idea for you to follow, but you will understand it better if you look at the drawings in Figure 3.3. When you look at (a), it is most likely that you will recognise a three-dimensional model of a cube. It is possible for you to see it as a two-dimensional pattern made up of a series of triangles, trapezoids and a square, but this is an unnecessarily complex interpretation and so you opt for the simpler, more familiar three-dimensional interpretation. As far as (b) is concerned, you probably again see the simplest interpretation which is as a two-dimensional drawing of a six-sided figure divided into six sections. However, it is possible, but much less immediately obvious, to perceive it as a three-dimensional cube if you focus on the mid-point of the drawing.

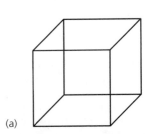 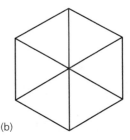

(a)   (b)

Figure 3.3 **An example of the Law of Prägnanz**

Some of the other Gestalt principles of grouping are included in Table 3.1.

Table 3.1		
Law	Definition	Example
Proximity	Elements that are physically close tend to be grouped together as a unit.	The written text on this page forms rows rather than columns because each letter is nearer to the letters to the right and left than to the letters above and below.
Similarity	Similar elements tend to be grouped together.	You see the **words in bold** as forming a separate group and different from the words in normal print.
Good continuation	Elements arranged in either straight or smoothly curving lines tend to be seen as a unit.	If you look at the cables going from your television set and your video machine to the socket in the wall, they might cross one another, but you still perceive them as two separate cords following a smooth path.
Closure	When a figure has a gap, we still tend to perceive it as a complete, closed figure.	If you read a piece of handwritten text, you will still 'see' a complete 'o' even if the pen has not formed a complete circle.
Common fate	Elements that move in the same direction tend to be perceived as a unit.	Cars travelling in one direction down a street will be perceived as a separate group from those going in the other direction.

Evaluation

You may be thinking that the Gestalt principles are little more than common sense. You know perfectly well that the letters on this page are grouped into words (law of proximity) and that words printed in bold stand out as separate from the rest of the text (law of similarity) and you probably feel that you do not need a law of organisation to tell you that this is so. The Gestalt laws seem simply to reflect the day-to-day regularities of our environment. The laws might seem so obvious to us simply because we have become very good at perceiving these regularities. The Gestalt laws, in spite of their apparent simplicity, tell us how our perceptions usually fit in with our expectations about the world. Gestalt principles have continued to influence psychologists who are interested in the perception of form. Indeed, as recently as 1990, Rock and Palmer added a new law (the law of connectedness) to the Gestalt set. Gestalt organisational principles also influenced the computational approach discussed in Chapter 2. However, there are problems with this approach and they are summarised as follows:

- Gestalt psychologists described perceptual organisation but did not really explain the underlying mechanisms. They suggested an innate, neurological explanation that involved electromagnetic fields in the brain but this idea was not well developed and has not been supported by research.
- They adopted a **phenomenological approach** which means that observers looked at their own immediate experience and then attempted to describe it. This method is no longer seen as scientifically valid. However, there have been a few later attempts to demonstrate some of the central Gestalt principles in controlled experiments. Navon (1977), for example, showed that we tend to perceive whole figures before we analyse the component parts. Weisstein and Wong (1986) demonstrated that we analyse the fine detail within the figure of a visual display whereas analysis of the ground is more global.
- Gestalt laws are rather vague and are sometimes difficult to distinguish one from another. The basic law of simplicity is quite hard to define and the simplest interpretation of an ambiguous figure is not always easy to predict.

- Many of the illustrations of organisation apply to very simple stimuli. Complex scenes involving everyday perception do not easily fit into a model based on simple two-dimensional illustrations.
- Eysenck and Keane (1995) suggest that the processes proposed by the Gestalt psychologists probably account only for the early stages of perceptual processing which will be organised later by previous experience.

Perceptual constancies

Constancy is the tendency for qualities of objects to stay the same despite changes in the way we view them. This is an important facet of visual perception. Try to imagine what it would be like if our perceptions were based purely on the image falling on the retina (the **proximal stimulus**). As you walked along the road towards a post box, it would appear to grow larger. As you moved your arm, your round wrist-watch would appear to change into an elliptical shape. As you moved from natural sunlight outdoors into artificial light indoors, your white shirt would appear yellow. Fortunately for us, our perceptual system seems to ensure that, in most circumstances our **distal stimulus** (our perceptual experience of objects 'out there') remains the same regardless of changes in the proximal stimulus.

Size constancy

This is our ability to see objects as remaining more or less the same size as we move closer or further away. The proximal size of an object can shrink and expand, but the distal size of the object seems to stay about the same. If a 6 ft. man walks away from you, you continue to perceive him as man-sized, regardless of his distance from you. It is interesting that this ability to maintain size constancy disappears under certain circumstances. When we look down from a plane, for example, cars and houses really do look like miniatures. When we take a holiday photo of a glorious, panoramic view, we can be quite disappointed with the result. In the photo, those majestic mountains can look quite pathetic. The camera, unlike the human perceiver, only registers angular size and does not compensate for the size changes that are related to distance changes. Our own size constancy mechanism does not appear to work as well when we view pictures as compared to real objects.

We have referred to a 'size-constancy mechanism', but psychologists cannot agree exactly what factors are involved. Several factors have been proposed and they are summarised below.

- *Familiarity.* If you know how big a lamp-post is, then you can usually guess its size regardless of how far away it is. This cannot be the only explanation however, because size constancy also seems to operate with unfamiliar objects.
- *Size-distance invariance.* According to this hypothesis, the observer calculates an object's perceived size (the distal view) by combining information about the object's retinal size (the proximal view) and its perceived distance. According to Rock (1983), this is a rapid, unconscious process, so you would not be aware of making these calculations.
- *Relative size.* When we judge the size of an object, we are doing so in the context of other surrounding objects. If you look at a book on your desk and then get up and walk across the room, the retinal image of the book will get smaller. However, the image of the desk will also get proportionately smaller so the ratio of the retinal sizes of the two objects remains constant. According to this explanation, then, objects seem to stay the same size as we move around because they maintain the same size relative to other objects around them.
- *Direct perception.* This explanation comes from Gibson's direct theory of perception (see Chapter 2). The first three factors listed above suggest that the mechanisms for size constancy are located within the viewer and depend on experience. According to the direct theory, on the other hand, the explanation is located within the stimulus, i.e. we can judge the size of an object by comparing it to invariants (aspects of perception which persist over time and space) in the surrounding area. You can better understand this idea by carrying out a simple investigation. Find a large, flat surface that has a regular, textured pattern (e.g. a pavement or a tiled floor). Take two identical books or newspapers and place them on the floor at distances of approximately 1 m. and 5 m. away from you. Then go back to your starting point and look at them. Note that each book covers exactly the same number of texture units,

i.e. each book may cover x tiles; this coverage remains the same whether the book is close to you or far away.

It is probable that all four of these factors have a part to play in our ability to demonstrate size constancy.

Shape constancy

This refers to the constancy of the perceived shape of an object despite variations in its orientation. Think of a door as it is opening. At the start, when it is shut, the door produces a rectangular image. As the door swings open, its retinal image changes from a rectangle to a trapezoid and yet we do not think that the door has changed its shape.

Our perceptual system seems to compensate for distance changes in slant in a similar way to the compensation for distance changes in size constancy. Memory may play a part in shape constancy just as it probably does for size constancy. You know that a plate is round, for example, even when you push it away from you on the table and it produces an elliptical shape on your retina.

- According to the shape–slant invariance hypothesis, we make use of depth cues (see p. 51) to help us decide on the degree of slant and then combine this information with information about the object's retinal image shape. Thouless (1931), an early researcher into perception, found that shape constancy can only be preserved if the observer is able to take into account the slant or orientation of the object. When he removed all clues about orientation, viewers' ability to conserve shape seemed to disappear.

If you look at two drawings – one a completely black oval shape and the other of the same oval shape but with shading that indicates depth – it is likely that you will perceive the black object as an elliptical pill or a sweet but will interpret the one with markings as being a circle viewed from an angle. This is because there are clues available to help us understand the object's orientation. In normal, everyday viewing conditions of three-dimensional objects, we have plenty of clues about orientation and so shape constancy usually works well.

Brightness (or lightness) constancy

This means that an object appears to stay the same brightness regardless of the amount of light falling on it. The white paper in this book will look equally bright to you whether you are reading it indoors, or outdoors in bright sunshine. However, the amount of light reflected from the page would be perhaps as much as a hundred times more if you were looking at it outside on a very sunny day. The fact that we perceive the page as equally bright under such different levels of illumination suggests that our perception of brightness does not relate to the amount of light reflected from the object but on the *percentage* of light reflected. While the amount of reflection can change vastly depending on the illumination, the percentage remains the same. This is called the object's **albedo**. Objects that look black to us have very low albedo (they reflect back about 5% of the light falling on them). Objects that appear to be various shades of grey have intermediate albedos (10 to 70% of the light is reflected back). Objects with high albedos (80 to 90% of the light is reflected back) are perceived as white.

As with the other constancies, there are probably several factors which contribute to brightness constancy. The most commonly accepted explanation is the ratio principle first developed by Wallach (1948). According to this principle, the observer notes the relative lightness of an object rather than its absolute lightness. In other words, we think that a white cat in moonlit conditions looks bright because it is the brightest object in sight. Similarly, a black dog looks very dark in bright sunlight because it is the darkest object in sight.

Colour constancy

This means that the colour of an object remains the same regardless of changes in the wavelength of the light falling on the object. Colour constancy does not seem quite as robust as some of the other constancies discussed so far. Hurvich (1981) found that clothes bought in shops with fluorescent lighting did not appear to be the same colour under tungsten lights at home. However, although colour constancy is not perfect, it rarely breaks down to the extent that an observer gives the same object two completely different colour names just because the illumination changes. A red dress in a shop is usually still perceived as red at home, even if the exact shade appears different. Colour perception is a complex area and the ways in which we maintain colour constancy are not yet fully understood, although it seems likely that several factors contribute.

Position constancy

When we walk around, the image of the world impinging on the retinal surface moves in an orderly and systematic fashion. For example, if you move your head to the right, the retinal image of all stationary objects slides across the retinal surface to the left. However, despite the fact that the retinal image moves, we do not experience the world as moving. Stationary objects seem to remain in a constant position regardless of our own movement. This is known as position constancy, and seems to be partly dependent on feedback from the muscles and from the organs of balance in the middle ear. Think of when you spin around and become dizzy – when you stop, the objects around you seem to be moving.

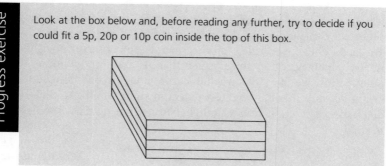

Look at the box below and, before reading any further, try to decide if you could fit a 5p, 20p or 10p coin inside the top of this box.

Most people believe that at least one of these coins would fit but, if you try placing even the smallest of these coins (i.e. the 5p piece) flat on its face into the box, you will find that it overlaps the sides. Try to explain in terms of size and shape constancy why people first believe that the coin will fit.

Depth cues

The image that falls on our retina is two-dimensional and yet we manage to perceive the world as three-dimensional. This seems to depend on using certain cues which give us information about depth and distance. There are two main types of cue:

- **Binocular cues** (dependent on the interaction of both eyes)
- **Monocular cues** (available to each eye acting independently)

Binocular cues

Our two eyes are approximately 6 to 7 cm. apart. This means that each eye receives slightly different images. This difference is called **retinal disparity**. You can demonstrate this disparity yourself. Close your left eye and then hold out a pen in front of you and align it with a distant vertical line (e.g. the vertical edge of a window or a door). Close the other eye and open the left and the pen will seem to have moved. The image from one eye usually dominates overall perception (in a right-handed person, the right is usually dominant). Eye dominance can easily be determined if you align the pen again – this time with both eyes open. Close each eye in turn and you will find that the pen appears to shift more with one eye closed than the other. If the greatest shift occurs with the right eye closed, then you are right-eye dominant and vice versa.

Although we receive two different images via our two eyes, we do not usually see double images. Our brain appears to be able to fuse the two images and this is called **stereopsis**. The brain uses this information about the differences in position of an object in the two images to give the impression of depth. The greater the difference in the position of the object, the nearer it is.

Convergence

Binocular vision provides another cue to depth in the form of convergence. The nearer an object is, the more the eyes have to turn inwards in order to focus on that object. Information from the orbital muscles which turn the eyes is therefore available as a further cue to depth.

The two binocular cues described above depend on the interaction of both eyes. They both result from processes and structures which are inherent in human beings. They do not appear to be dependent on learning or experience. For this reason, they are called 'primary cues'. It is obviously beneficial to human beings to use both eyes to process visual information. For example, common tasks involving judgements of relative depth (e.g. threading a needle, inserting coins into slots, etc.) are performed 30% faster and more accurately using both eyes than just one eye (Sheedy *et al.*, 1986). However, if some-one loses the sight of one eye or has one eye closed, it is still possible to make judgements about depth. This must mean that some depth cues are available to one eye working alone. These are called monocular cues.

Monocular cues

There are several monocular cues but only one is a primary cue (i.e. one that is independent of learning). This is accommodation. In order to focus on objects at different distances from the eye, the lens has to change. This occurs because of the movements of the muscles holding the lens in place. (These are **autonomic responses** and are not under conscious control.) The amount of accommodation of the lens provides feedback to the brain about the distance of the fixated object. However, according to Hochberg (1971), accommodation provides a fairly weak cue to distance. In any case, the process of accommodation only works over short distances. Anything further away than approximately 25 ft. is set at optical infinity (which simply means that no further change can occur in the shape of the lens) and so there must be other cues available. The remaining cues are called pictorial monocular cues (they seem to depend on properties of the image itself rather than on the physiology of the visual system). they are often used by artists to create the illusion of depth in flat, two-dimensional pictures. It seems likely that these cues are learned through experience with our visual environment and, for this reason, are sometimes called secondary cues. They are described below.

- *Overlap or Superimposition.* If one object overlaps and appears to cut off the view of another, we assume that the first object is nearer (Figure 3.4).

Figure 3.4 **An example of overlap or superimposition**

This cue only works for relative depth so, in Figure 3.4, you can only say that the circle is nearer than the triangle but not how far away the circle is from you.

- *Relative size.* In an array of similar objects, it is assumed that smaller ones are further away. Retinal image size is an important cue for direct perception and computational theories. It is also important for constructivist theories because of experience with **familiar size** (e.g. a very small elephant would be assumed to be far away).

- *Height in the visual field (elevation).* Objects placed higher up in the visual field seem to be further away. This cue depends on the relationship to the horizon. Look at Figure 3.5. Post (b) seems further away because its base is closer to the horizon (i.e. higher in the plane). The reverse holds true for targets above the horizon. Bird (c) seems further away than bird (d) because it is lower in the picture plane.

- *Texture gradient.* Gibson (1950) suggested a way of combining linear perspective and relative size information into one cue which he called texture gradient. Texture or grain appears to become finer or smoother as distance becomes greater (see Chapter 2).

- *Linear perspective.* This is a well-known pictorial depth cue which gives the effect of parallel lines appearing to converge as they recede into the distance (e.g. rail tracks or roads).

- *Aerial perspective.* Objects with clear and distinct images are seen as being closer to you, whereas distant images seem hazy and indistinct. This effect is usually observed in broad landscapes and city scenes. Distant mountains, woods or buildings seem blurred, bluish and hazy in comparison to nearby objects.

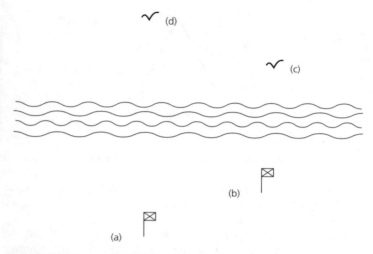

Figure 3.5 **An example of height in the visual field**

- *Shadowing*. Light usually travels in straight lines so, if we are viewing an object with an ingoing dent and the light source is above, the lower part of the dent will catch the light whereas the upper part will be in shadow.

  If the shadow is reversed, the same pattern will be seen as an outgoing bump and it will look as if we are viewing the object from below. Shadowing is often used by artists and sign-writers to give the impression of three-dimensional words or pictures standing out from their background.

- *Motion parallax*. So far we have only considered depth cues which involve stable objects that can also be represented in a picture or photo (pictorial cues) but, if we add motion to the incoming visual pattern, we provide additional opportunities for depth cues to appear. If we are moving, objects close to us appear to move faster than objects further away. For example, if we are in a train, the apparent movement of distant objects is slower than closer objects (e.g. telegraph poles next to the line).

  A special form of motion parallax occurs when an object moves or rotates. The relative pattern of movement of parts of the object can give us the information about its three-dimensional shape. This is referred to as **kinetic depth effect**.

Try to draw a picture that incorporates all the pictorial distance cues and label them.

Visual illusions

Everything we have considered in the previous two sections of this chapter has contributed to our understanding of veridical perception (i.e. perception which matches the actual physical stimulus). However, we sometimes have to make perceptual judgements under poor visual conditions, and consequently we are liable to make mistakes. Psychologists are interested in perceptual errors because they can provide useful clues about the normal functioning of the visual system. Although visual illusions can occur in the natural environment, most of the illusions studied by psychologists have been specially devised.

Richard Gregory (see Chapter 2) has taken a particular interest in visual illusions and has identified four different types:

- ambiguous figures
- paradoxical figures
- fictitious figures
- distortions

Gregory saw visual perception as an active process of using information to suggest and test hypotheses. He believed that we used information about size and distance in order to make perceptual judgements, but that, in the absence of such clues, we have to make the best guess about what we are seeing.

Ambiguous figures

Examples of ambiguous figures can be seen on p. 27 (the Necker Cube) and on p. 42 (the Rubin Vase). Gregory believes that we switch between two equally plausible interpretations of these figures because there is no surrounding context to make one hypothesis more convincing than the other (see p. 27 for a fuller explanation).

Paradoxical figures

At first sight, the drawing in Figure 3.6 seems to be of a normal elephant. However, if you look closely, you will see that this drawing is 'impossible' – it could not be produced as a three-dimensional object. This description is the basis for the explanation. Constructivists like Gregory believe that people educated in Western culture are so used to interpreting two-dimensional line drawings as three-dimensional real objects that they do this automatically. Someone trying to make sense of the example in Figure 3.6 in this way finds that a three-dimensional model will not work and so is puzzled by the picture.

Figure 3.6 **A paradoxical figure**

Fictitious figures

Look at Figure 3.7. There is a very strong illusion of a white triangle standing out in the front of the drawing even though this triangle has no explicitly drawn contours. For this reason, this kind of illusion is sometimes known as an **illusory contour**. Coren and Porac (1983) have suggested that we see simple, familiar figures in preference to meaningless, disorganised parts. This suggestion fits in with the Gestalt Law of Prägnanz (see p. 43) and also what we know about depth cues, i.e. a white triangle in front of three black circles 'explains' the apparent wedges cut out of the circles (i.e. the triangle is simply obscuring parts of the circles). This kind of explanation suggests that the experience of illusory contours depends on top-down processing and there is experimental evidence to support this view (Coren and Porac, 1983). However, it is not universally accepted, and Meyer and Petry (1987) reviewed several other attempts to explain this kind of visual illusion, including some bottom-up approaches. One such suggestion is that illusory contours are caused by simultaneous lightness contrast. This means that the illusory triangle in Figure 3.7 stands out as a separate area of brightness in contrast to the black of the partial circles. However, this view is disputed by Rock (1986) because there are figures which have all the necessary elements to produce the lightness contrast but which do not give rise to illusory contours. It seems, then, that there is currently no satisfactory explanation of illusory contours that accounts for all the data.

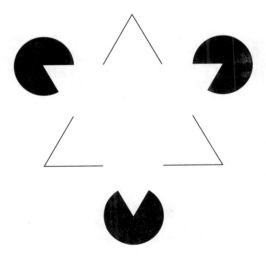

Figure 3.7 **A fictitious figure**

Distortions

There are several well-known visual illusions that fall into this category. The one that has attracted the most attention is probably the Müller-Lyer illusion (see Figure 3.8(a)), so we shall concentrate on that. This is a powerful illusion in which the line with the outward fins is perceived as longer than the line with the inward fins, even though they are exactly the same length.

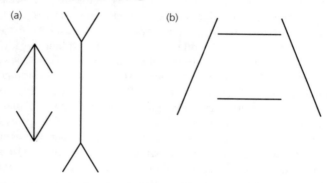

Figure 3.8 (a) The Müller-Lyer illusion; (b) The Ponzo Illusion

Gregory has explained this illusion in terms of misapplied constancy scaling. Size constancy scaling means that the viewer makes length judgements on the basis of size constancy so that a line that looks further away will be judged as longer. Gregory suggests that this mechanism which helps us to maintain stable size perception in the real three-dimensional world could lead us to misinterpret two-dimensional drawings. He says that the Müller-Lyer lines are perceived as simple perspective drawings of three-dimensional objects.

This theory has been supported by empirical evidence. For example, Pedersen and Wheeler (1983) investigated the illusion with two groups of American Navajo Indians. One group had lived all their lives in typically Western architecture (i.e. rectangular buildings with outside edges and inside corners). The other group had been brought up in typical, round Navajo houses and were not used to the carpentered environment of Western houses. Pedersen and Wheeler found that the Navajos in the first group were significantly more susceptible to the illusion.

However, Gregory's theory has not gone unchallenged. DeLucia and Hochberg (1991) have shown that the Müller-Lyer illusion still occurs where there are no depth cues. They stood wooden models shaped like the fins on the floor (see Figure 3.9).

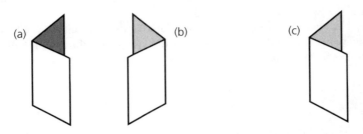

Figure 3.9 Stimuli similar to those used by DeLucia and Hochberg (1991)

The distance between (a) and (b) is the same as between (b) and (c), and yet the distance appears larger just as it does in the two-dimensional version of the Müller-Lyer. It is quite obvious in this three-dimensional version that the spaces between the two sets of fins are not at different depths (i.e. **misapplied size constancy** cannot be working here) and yet the illusion persists.

Coren (1981) suggested that the illusion can be explained in terms of eye-movement patterns. He showed that the eyes track a longer path in the line with the fins pointing outwards than in the one with the inward fins and thus we judge the former line to be longer than the latter.

Day (1989) has put forward the conflicting cues theory which states that two factors are involved in our perception of the length of the lines.

1. the actual length of the vertical lines
2. the overall length of the figure

Day believes that, in the case of the Müller-Lyer illusion (see Figure 3.8(a)), there is a conflict between these two cues and so a compromise perception of length is generated. The overall length of the outward fins version is larger and so the estimation of the vertical shaft is also judged to be slightly larger. This idea fits with data from a study by Coren and Girgus (1972), in which they showed participants the illusion where the fins were drawn in a different colour from the shafts. They reasoned that the fins would be less likely to be taken into consideration if they were coloured and, therefore, not a uniform part of the overall figure. Under these circumstances, the shafts were usually seen as being the same length, i.e. the fins no longer acted as distractors.

As you can see, there is no satisfactory explanation which accounts for all the distortion illusions and each illusion probably arises from a combination of factors.

Progress exercise

Look at the Ponzo illusion in Figure 3.8(b) and try to explain, in terms of misapplied size constancy scaling, why the upper horizontal bar appears to be longer than the lower bar.

Pattern perception (object recognition)

To recognise something means that we match incoming visual stimuli with information stored in our long-term memory. We are usually very good at differential object recognition, but psychologists have found it quite difficult to explain this ability fully. Consider T t *t* *T* T **T** – you will have no difficulty in recognising them all as the letter 't' and yet they are different in size, typeface, orientation, etc. Any plausible theory of pattern recognition needs to be able to explain this ability to recognise the same pattern represented in different guises. There have been many theories of pattern recognition but we shall only look at a few. References are given at the end of this chapter for books which will provide a fuller picture.

Template matching

The simplest view is to suppose that the perceptual stimulus is processed and then matched against a number of copies or templates which are stored in memory. The template that gives the best fit is the one that the system will choose and the object is then recognised. This works well for stimuli that have little variation and is the basis for many coding systems used in everyday life. For example, the distinctively shaped digits printed on the bottom of cheques and the bar codes on supermarket products are read by computers using the template-matching method. Although template matching can work well for a computer scanning numbers and lines, it is too inflexible to account for the complexity of human pattern recognition.

Another problem is the sheer size of the memory needed to store millions of templates of objects. Each object can be presented in many different orientations and you would soon run into storage problems if pattern perception were nothing more than a template-matching process. In any case, template models could only explain our recognition of very simple patterns and not the complex visual scenes which we constantly have to interpret in everyday life.

Prototype models

These are more flexible versions of template-matching theories. A prototype is an abstract, idealised pattern which is stored in our memories. Whenever we see an object, we compare it to a stored prototype. If we do not find an immediate match, we continue comparing with other prototypes until we find one that fits. The prototype does not have to be an exact fit as long as the match is reasonably close. You would therefore recognise your best friend coming down the street towards you regardless of whether he or she was wearing unusual clothes, had a new hair-style or had suddenly started wearing glasses because he or she would match the broad, 'best friend' prototype stored in your memory.

This approach is more flexible and economical than template matching, and also accounts for our ability to recognise objects in spite of their precise representation or orientation and however fragmented they are. However, it does not explain the underlying physiological mechanisms or how the prototypes are stored in memory.

Feature theories

These theories assume that the first stage of perception involves processing the image in terms of its basic features. An early theory devised by Selfridge (1959) is the pandemonium model, which consists of a set of sub-programs designed to search for a specific feature. Selfridge described this model using the analogy of a group of *demons* contributing to each stage of feature analysis.

Imagine looking at the letter E. The first demon (image demon) represents this as a pattern of light falling on the retina. At the next level are line demons which search for a particular line (e.g. vertical, horizontal, curved, etc.). If its line is present, the vertical line demon will 'shout'. Other demons will also shout, but the volume of the shout depends on how prominent their particular line is in the letter. Thus for a capital E, the horizontal line demon will probably shout the loudest. Next, the angle demons collate information from the line demons and look for the particular angle that they represent. If they find it, they, too, will shout to the next level (pattern demons). The pattern demons then analyse all the information that has been passed on from the angle demons. It is possible at this stage for the F demon and the E demon (and possibly also the L) to be shouting simultaneously, but the accumulated information from all the demons favours the E, so it is the E demon that shouts loudest to the decision demon and is finally recognised.

This model is called the pandemonium model to reflect the uncertainty of feature processing. Many letters have similar features (e.g. M, N, W) and so they may set off many of the demons causing a pandemonium of shouting. It may seem quite an odd idea to have a host of demons shrieking away inside our heads, but it is only intended as a metaphor for the processes involved in feature detection.

There is some support for this kind of model from both psychological and physiological evidence. Garner (1979) found that people need more time to distinguish between letters that share many features in common (e.g. P, R, B) than to distinguish between dissimilar letters like Z and O. This suggests that some kind of stage-by-stage feature analysis takes place when we recognise letters.

Biological evidence comes from Hubel and Wiesel (1959), who carried out a series of experiments where they implanted small wires called micro-electrodes into single cells in the visual cortex of cats. They found cortical cells that were selectively sensitive to different patterns of light. Some responded to vertical bars of light, others to horizontal and diagonal bars. These cells are called **feature detector**

cells because they seem to respond to particular features like edges and corners in the environment. It seems then that we have special feature detectors wired in to help us with pattern recognition – at least, for letters of the alphabet and other simple patterns. However, there are problems with the feature detection theories.

The feature detection theories simply list a set of features found in a stimulus, but they do not describe the relationship between features and parts of objects. Think about the letter T – in terms of features, this consists of one vertical line and one horizontal line but this description is not enough to identify it. Consider the symbols in Figure 3.10. All of these figures meet the criteria for a feature-based description of a T but none of them depict a real T. We also need to know the structural description – that is, how the component features are configured and connected. Another problem is that feature detection theory also makes no allowance for the fact that, in many patterns, some features are more important than others. As with template-matching theories, feature theory is too simplistic to explain how we recognise more complex objects. It cannot explain how we recognise faces or everyday objects like a telephone.

Figure 3.10 **A figure to illustrate feature detection theories**

The next approach that we shall look at specifically addresses this question of how we recognise more complex objects.

Computational theories

This type of theory has elements of both the prototype and the distinctive features approach. Computational theories differ in that they aim to develop computer-based programs that can simulate some of the perceptual tasks carried out by human beings. One of these tasks, which has been a main focus of interest for computational theories, is the rapid, accurate recognition of three-dimensional objects. You will remember from Chapter 2 that Marr was one of the most influential, computational theorists. Look back to p. 34 for a summary of his stages of object recognition. Marr believed that most objects, even quite complicated ones, could be represented in terms of simpler structures like cones and cylinders. At the three-dimensional representation stage, the visual system has to work out where the major axes of the figures lie and then deduce how the object and its parts are arranged around these axes. Consider the consequence of combining small cylinder-shaped blocks. Using six cylinders (of different sizes) can construct a representation of a two-legged creature or a recognisable human figure (Figure 3.11).

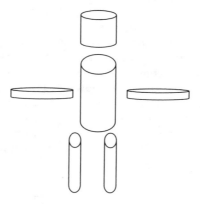

Figure 3.11 **Combinations of cylinders can be used to represent the shapes of various creatures. After Marr and Nishihara (1978)**

A more recent computational approach is the recognition-by-components theory (RBC) put forward by Biederman (1987, 1990). He believed that an object can be represented as a configuration of simple shapes called geons. He proposed 36 different geons which can be flexibly and economically combined to form various objects. According to Biederman, three geons usually provide enough information for accurate object recognition and it is possible to construct more than 150 million objects from various combinations of three geons taken from the pool of 36. Sometimes only two are needed, and the same two can be used in different configurations to represent a range of objects (see Figure 3.12).

Biederman's own research (1987) suggests that RBC accounts well for human shape recognition and that, using geon identification,

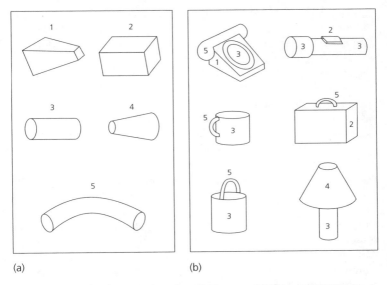

Figure 3.12 **Objects as configurations of geons (Biederman, 1990) reproduced with permission from MIT Press**

objects are recognised even when the object is highly complex, degraded and presented without much detail. His theory has not yet been widely tested by other researchers but some interesting studies have been done. Cave and Kosslyn (1993) suggested that human beings may encode the overall shape of an object and only identify the constituent parts afterwards. They gave participants drawings like the ones in Figure 3.13 and asked them to identify the objects as quickly as possible.

As you can see, (a) shows a pair of scissors broken into geon-consistent parts while (b) shows an identical pair of scissors chopped up more arbitrarily. Participants were equally fast and accurate for drawings in both conditions, which suggests that geon identification is not necessarily the most natural method for human perceivers.

Computational theories have been very important because they have provided a framework for theories of pattern recognition. However, there are clear differences between human and computer processing. Computers have a limited set of stored representations whereas human beings are believed to have an infinite capacity for storage. Human

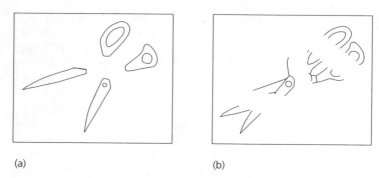

(a)   (b)

Figure 3.13 **Drawings similar to those used by Cave and Kosslyn (1993) with permission from Pion Limited, London**

recognition usually occurs extremely fast and accurately, whereas computer-based recognition systems are relatively slow and inflexible. RBC is a promising approach and seems to meet many of the requirements for object recognition more satisfactorily than Marr's proposals. However, more research is needed before it can be accepted as an accurate account of human object perception.

Perceiving movement

One problem of computational approaches is that they focus mainly on the perception of stationary objects. Yet, as we know, both objects and observers move around in the normal environment and human perception is adept at coping with this. For many animals, the perception of movement can be crucial for survival but, for humans, too, it seems to provide important sources of information.

Our tendency to respond to real movement is so powerful that the visual system sometimes picks up apparent movement where none is present. One example of this is the **stroboscopic effect** first demonstrated systematically by the Gestalt psychologist, Max Wertheimer (1912). He flashed a light on and off in a darkened room and then, after a 50-millisecond delay, flashed a light on and off again at a point slightly to the right of the first light. It appears to observers that the light has moved through space between the two points. This phenomenon is called **apparent movement** because there is no real movement – there is simply one light flashing on and off followed by another light flashing on and off. Flashing disco lights that appear to follow each other make use of this illusion. Films and animated cartoons represent another example of stroboscopic movement. There is no real movement in films – it is simply an illusion created by recording a series of still photographs (frames) on film and running them very rapidly through a projector. As you can see, this effect has many practical applications but, for psychologists, it shows that a key stimulus for the visual system is relative displacement over time. The brain will perceive that an object has moved if it is in one place and, then, shortly afterwards, appears to be in another.

There are other illusions of movement such as the **autokinetic effect** where a stationary pinpoint of light in a darkened room appears to the observer to move. Induced movement is something you have probably often experienced. Induced movement occurs in situations where the movement of one object induces the perception of movement in another object. A good example is when you are sitting on a train waiting for it to pull out of the station. If a train alongside you at the next platform starts to pull out first, you have the strong feeling that it is your train which is moving. This feeling is only dispelled once the train has gone.

These examples should indicate to you that movement perception is a highly complex activity. Many theories have been put forward to explain the perception of movement, whether real or apparent. There are several physiological explanations, but it is beyond the scope of this book to discuss them. Further reading is suggested at the end of this chapter. We shall look briefly at psychological explanations which we will divide into two types.

The effect of the environment

Gibson, and others who favour the direct perception approach, believed that the environment is rich with information about movement. Gibson distinguished between two aspects of motion perception.

- *Local movement signal* – some things move in the environment while others stay stationary.
- *Global optical flow* – all elements in the scene are moving.

Imagine sitting on a park bench and staring at a statue in the lake when a child runs across in front of your view. With your eyes fixed on the distant statue, the running child provides a local movement signal by rapidly covering and uncovering parts of the stationary background. Even if you were to turn your attention to the child and follow her with your eyes so that her image remains stationary on your retina, her image still covers and uncovers the static background. So, for Gibson, the vital information needed for movement perception is the local motion of the moving object relative to its background. Now imagine that you get up, start to walk along the path and pass a woman sitting on the next bench. You are moving, and so the images of both the stationary woman and the static background slide across your retina. According to Gibson, this causes a global optic flow which provides you with the information that it is *you* who is moving and not the stationary woman or the background. This explanation seems to work well in this kind of situation but does not account for the autokinetic effect. However, Gibson, as an ecological researcher, criticised artificial laboratory experiments and felt that it was only necessary to explain real-life perception.

Monocular depth cues (see p. 52) like relative size, motion parallax and the kinetic depth effect are also helpful in detecting motion.

The effect of context

It seems that human perceivers take context into account when judging object movement. Ramachandran and Anstis (1986) presented participants with two crosses (see Figure 3.14(a)) and showed them rapidly, one after the other. Participants reported seeing the crosses moving in either a clockwise or anti-clockwise direction. When the presentation was changed so that an extra initial cross was inserted before the sequence of the original two (see Figure 3.14(b)), participants all reported seeing the movement as clockwise. This suggests that observers believe that movement will usually continue in the direction it first started. (Note that this fits in well with the Gestalt law of good continuation for static two-dimensional images; see p. 44).

Another interesting study which supports the effect of context was conducted by Shiffar and Freyd (1993). They tested the concept of the shortest path constraint. This means that, when one stimulus is rapidly alternated with another, apparent movement occurs along the shortest possible route even though many other, longer routes

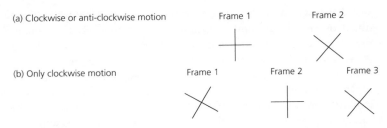

Figure 3.14 Stimuli similar to those used by Ramachandran and Anstis (1986). From *Sensation and Perception*, 5th edition, by E.B. Goldstein. © 1999. Reprinted with permission of Wadsworth, a division of Thomson Learning. Fax 800 730-2215)

would be possible. They used two photos of a young woman with her fists held out in front of her. In the first photo, the arms were held out fairly straight in front of her but, in the second photo, her arms were crossed. These photos were then alternated rapidly in front of observers so that the arms would appear to be moving. The shortest path constraint would predict that the viewers would see the arms moving *through* one another. However, participants actually reported seeing one arm going *underneath* the other (i.e. a longer route). This suggests that participants understood that the first interpretation was physically impossible and so rejected the path that would normally have been chosen in favour of the longer one.

This kind of evidence suggests that there is some effect of context on our perception of motion, although it is not yet entirely clear what mechanisms underlie this.

Summary

In this chapter, we have looked at various ways in which we organise our perceptions. One early suggestion came from the Gestalt psychologists who formulated a set of laws to explain how we group together elements of a picture to form a perceptual whole. Gestalt ideas have been quite influential but they lack explanatory power. Another way that we maintain a stable, organised view of the world is by means of perceptual constancy. This helps us to maintain size, shape, colour, etc. even when objects in our visual environment are shifting and changing. Depth cues help us to convert the two-dimensional image that falls on our retina into the three-dimensional image that we actually perceive. These become more effective when they are used in combination, although they sometimes lead us into misperceptions when we are presented with two-dimensional visual illusions. Pattern recognition was the final topic to be covered. Various theories have been put forward to explain how we recognise objects, but so far, none have been able to account for the ease and speed with which human beings can recognise a huge variety of objects regardless of their shape, size and orientation.

Review exercise

Complete the following table summarising theories of pattern recognition.

Theory	Supporting evidence	Evalutation

Further reading

Bruce, V. and Green, P.R. (1992) *Visual Perception: Physiology, Psychology and Ecology*, 2nd edn, Hove and London: Lawrence Erlbaum Associates. This is a comprehensive text which covers a range of topics beyond the A-level syllabus. It is clearly written and reasonably accessible for A-level students who wish to explore the topics in this chapter in greater detail.

Eysenck, M. and Keane, M. (1995) *Cognitive Psychology: A Student's Handbook*, 3rd edn, Hove: Psychology Press. Provides a broad coverage of all the issues covered in this chapter. It is clearly set out and easy to read.

Roth, I. and Bruce, V. (1995) *Perception and Representation: Current Issues*, 2nd edn, Buckingham: Open University Press. Provides an up-to-date and in-depth treatment of some of the issues covered in this chapter and is particularly helpful on object recognition. It is a text intended for undergraduates, but it is written in a fairly accessible style.

4

Perceptual development

Introduction

So far in this book, we have been considering the perceptual capacities of a normally sighted, human adult. However, it seems clear that changes occur in perception as an individual develops, matures and learns from experience. Some of these changes lead to a more accurate representation of the physical environment, but it also appears that certain perceptual abilities deteriorate with age. For example, thickening of the lens (see Chapter 1) with age can affect colour perception (particularly blue/green and white/yellow distinctions) and, together with reduced pupil size in the ageing eye, limits the amount of light reaching the retina and so reduces sensitivity (Corso, 1981). There is also substantial age-related loss of neurons in the visual cortex which can cause a reduction in **visual acuity** (Weale, 1986). All of these changes are examples of perceptual development.

However, psychologists have been particularly interested in the perceptual capacities of human beings when they first come into the world as babies.

There has been a long-standing philosophical debate about how and when our perceptual abilities develop. At one extreme, **nativists** believe that we are born with certain perceptual abilities, and that, although these abilities are sometimes incomplete or immature at birth, they develop through a process of *maturation* which is genetically programmed and does not rely on learning. At the other extreme, **empiricists** believe that a child develops perceptual abilities through experience of the environment. Contemporary psychologists would be unlikely to subscribe to either of these extreme views and are more likely to see perceptual abilities arising from a mixture of environmental and innate factors.

The aim of this chapter is to present some of the evidence concerning the development of visual perception and to evaluate the various methods used to investigate this question.

Overview of methods

Neonate studies

The most obvious way of investigating the perceptual capacities of neonates (new-born infants) would seem to be by studying them directly. If perceptual abilities are innate, then we would expect to find them in neonates. If perceptual abilities are dependent on experience, then they would be absent in very young infants. However, the reality is not so straightforward and some studies can be difficult to interpret. Some of the difficulties of neonate research are outlined below:

- Babies produce only a limited range of observable behaviours. It might seem easy to demonstrate that a baby *cannot* do something. However, it could be that perceptual abilities are not being detected because infants are incapable of behaving in a way that demonstrates these abilities to the researcher.
- Some abilities such as accommodation (see Chapter 1) are not present at birth but develop during the first few months of life. However, this seems to depend on maturation processes rather than experience with the visual environment.

- Another problem concerns the difficulty of testing young babies. They sleep for long periods and quickly lose interest.
- Babies do not follow verbal instructions and cannot answer questions directly.

Researchers have found some ingenious methods for tackling these problems (see Table 4.1), but they cannot completely overcome them. For this reason, psychologists interested in the development of perception have looked at alternative sources of evidence. These are set out below.

Write a brief summary of the major difficulties associated with human neonate studies.

Progress exercise

Non-human animal studies

There are several ways in which animals have been used in perceptual studies, but the most common technique is to deprive them of some aspect of normal sensory and perceptual stimulation and then to record the effects.

Advantages

- Using animals means that the researcher can manipulate the visual environment in ways that would not be permitted with human participants. (However, researchers still have to adhere to very strict ethical guidelines.)
- The shorter life span (and hence rapid development) of many animals also allows the researcher to study the long-term effects of visual deprivation more easily than is possible with human beings.
- Many animals are **precocial** (they are at a fairly late stage of development when they are born or hatched) which is useful in studies such as the visual cliff (see Figure 4.2) where human infants can only be used from the age of about 6 months.

Table 4.1 Some of the methods used to test human infants

Method	Description	Assumption
Eye-movement monitoring	Babies' eye movements are recorded photographically when they are scanning visual stimuli such as geometric shapes.	If the babies only focus on a single or limited number of features (e.g. the contours), it is assumed that the baby cannot perceive the whole figure.
Preferential looking (PL)	This is sometimes called *spontaneous visual preference technique (SPV)*. It involves the simultaneous presentation of two visual stimuli.	If the infant looks at one for longer than at the other, it is inferred that: 1. The baby can distinguish between the two. 2. The baby prefers one stimulus to the other.
Habituation	This is used when the researcher wants to know if the baby can distinguish between two stimuli when there is no visual preference for one of them. One stimulus is presented over and over again to the baby until she becomes so familiar with it (**habituates** to it) that she loses interest and stops looking. The researcher then presents a novel stimulus.	If the infant starts looking at the novel stimulus having habituated to the old one, the researcher concludes that she can tell the difference between the two.

Table 4.1 continued

Method	Description	Assumption
Sucking rate	The baby is given a dummy and the sucking rate is measured in response to different visual stimuli. After prolonged exposure to one stimulus, habituation will occur (i.e. the sucking rate will change). At this point, a novel stimulus is presented to see if the sucking rate changes again.	If there is a change in sucking rate when a novel stimulus is presented, it is assumed that the baby can distinguish between the two stimuli.
Conditioning a head-turning response	The baby is rewarded (e.g. by being shown a colourful toy; this is 'conditioning') every time it looks at a particular stimulus, and so quickly learns to turn towards it.	If the stimulus is then shown among other visual stimuli and the infant continues to indicate a preference for it, it is assumed that the baby can distinguish it.
Heart and breathing rate	The baby's heart and/or breathing rate is monitored for changes when novel stimuli are presented.	If there is a change in rate, the researcher concludes that the baby can recognise the new stimulus as being different.
Visually evoked potentials (VEPs)	Electrodes are attached to the baby's scalp to measure electrical activity in the brain. Certain patterns called VEPs occur in response to visual stimuli.	If *different* VEPs are recorded in response to *different* visual stimuli, it is assumed that the infant is distinguishing between them.

Disadvantages

- As with human neonates, animals cannot follow instructions or respond directly to questions. Researchers have to draw conclusions based solely on their observations.
- There is a problem with generalisation. While deprivation studies can provide useful information about the species being studied, it can be misleading to apply the findings to human beings because human behaviour is more affected by learning (or some other explanation).

Cataract studies

A cataract is a condition in which the lens becomes so cloudy that, in certain cases, it causes complete blindness. When the condition is present at birth, it is called a congenital cataract. Von Senden (1960), for example, has reported on studies where individuals, blind from birth, have acquired vision in adulthood through the surgical removal of cataracts. Studies of these patients provide a sort of natural experiment where humans have been deprived of vision through disease or congenital malformation but not through delib- erate intervention by an experimenter. Their experiences when they first acquire vision can give us information about which perceptual abilities are learned and which are innate. The assumption is that perceptual abilities which operate immediately after the surgery must be innate (evidence from cataract studies is looked at again on p. 88).

Advantages

- The main advantage of these studies is that they involve adults who can follow instructions and describe what is happening to them.
- The visual deprivation/distortion occurs naturally without any intervention from the researcher.

Disadvantages

- There have been only a relatively small number of such case studies reported and they have not all been investigated in the same way. Patients varied in age when they underwent surgery and not all of them were blind from birth.

- People who are deprived of sight frequently develop heightened awareness in other sensory modalities such as touch. When their sight is restored, they may continue to depend more on this other modality because of familiarity.
- Many of the individuals reported in these case studies were poorly prepared psychologically for their new visual experience of the world and became anxious and depressed. These emotional side-effects could have obscured their visual abilities.
- The visual system may have deteriorated over the years of not being able to see and be functioning in a restricted way which is not capable of improvement.

Readjustment studies

These studies involve adult human volunteers wearing special goggles which make the visual world appear different (e.g. by turning everything upside-down, by switching the left of the visual field to the right side and vice versa, etc.). Similar studies have also been carried out on animals. If individuals are able to adapt to a distorted world, it is assumed that learning plays a major role in the development of our perceptual abilities. If unable to adapt, it is assumed that perceptual abilities are innate and difficult to modify.

Advantages

- Participants are adults who can understand and respond and who can move freely about in their environment.

Disadvantages

- Adults have already had a great deal of experience in coping with the visual world and might have developed many strategies which are not available to babies. It is therefore difficult to generalise findings from these studies to explain how babies develop their perceptual abilities.
- There is a suggestion that adults wearing distorting goggles are not actually learning a new way of perceiving the world but are simply developing appropriate motor movements in order to

be able to continue to move around as safely and efficiently as possible.

Cross-cultural studies

These are studies which involve comparisons between human beings who are brought up in contrasting environments and social backgrounds. If there are variations in the perception of the same visual stimulus by such different groups, it would seem to offer a strong argument for the role of learning in perception.

Advantages

- These studies help to correct the balance in much psychological research which only looks at Western cultures to draw universal conclusions.

Disadvantages

- Most of the research has used two-dimensional illustrations as stimulus material. Preference for one stimulus over another may reflect artistic tradition within the two cultures rather than a genuine difference in perception.

Conclusion

You can see that there is no single method used to investigate the development of perception which is problem free. It is helpful to consider the evidence from all these areas in deciding how much of our perceptual ability is learned and how much is innate. We will consider some of the important findings from all of these sources in the following sections. However, evidence from cross-cultural studies, which can also, of course, be relevant to a discussion of cultural variations in perception, will be discussed in more detail in Chapter 5.

Evidence from neonate studies

It seems clear that the neonatal visual equipment is not fully mature at birth. Many of the characteristics of the adult system seem either to be present in the new-born or to develop in the first few months of life but the full adult pattern of response is not yet in place. For example, the infant does not have the visual acuity of adults, although this improves rapidly as the receptors in the fovea develop (at birth they can only focus on objects which are quite close). Focusing is difficult for the infant if the object is very close or too far away but, again, this ability develops rapidly. Babies sometimes move their two eyes in different directions instead of aligning the foveas of both eyes on an object. This probably reflects the fact that retinal-disparity-sensitive cells in the visual cortex are absent for the first few weeks of life (Aslin, 1988). Infants as young as 2 weeks will look at a moving stimulus in preference to a stationary one (Nelson and Horowitz, 1987) but cannot track the moving stimulus smoothly until about 10 weeks (Aslin, 1981). Infants appear to have brightness and colour vision at birth but discrimination performance improves within the first few months. In most of the examples given here, perceptual ability improves as the underlying physiological mechanisms mature.

We shall now look at three particular areas of neonate research:

- pattern recognition
- depth perception
- constancies

Pattern recognition

The PL technique (see Table 4.1) has been widely used to investigate pattern recognition in infancy. A pioneer of this technique was Fantz, who found that babies as young as 2 days old could distinguish between patterned and unpatterned figures although this fine discrimination continued to improve as the babies grew older (see Figure 4.1). He also found that 2 to 4-month-old babies prefer patterns to either colour or brightness. In later research, Fantz and Yeh (1979) found that babies show changes in their preferences as they mature. At first, they prefer simple patterns with highly contrasting elements but, by the age of 5 months, they prefer to look at objects with subtle variations in contrast.

One particular type of pattern perception which has attracted research is face recognition. Fantz (1961) believed that face recognition was innate in humans. He presented 4-day-old to 6-month-old babies with the stimuli shown in Figure 4.1. These stimuli consisted of flat, pink boards about the size and shape of an adult head with black patterns painted on them. As you can see, (a) is a schematic face, (b) has the same black features but randomly distributed and (c) has the same amount of black colouring but presented in a solid band. All babies showed a preference for stimulus (a) over (b) (although this preference was slight), while almost all the babies ignored stimulus (c). Fantz concluded from this study that face perception does not have to be learned and that human infants possess an innate preference for facedness.

Figure 4.1 **Stimulus pictures used for research into face recognition (after Fantz, 1961)**

However, several criticisms have been made of Fantz's experiment. The stimuli were highly artificial and did not resemble real faces. They were static, unlike human faces which are mobile and frequently change expression. Not all researchers have replicated Fantz's findings. Hershenson *et al.* (1965) used the same method but did not obtain the same results. Haith (1980) believed that infants in Fantz's study preferred the 'face' and the 'scrambled face' to the other one because they contained more contour. Contour detection is an important part of object recognition and Haith claims that this is also true for infants. This is supported by Flavell (1985), who found that babies, if shown objects that have the same amount of contour and movement, look at them for similar amounts of time, i.e. they show no preference for faces.

On the other hand, Goren *et al.* (1975) used slightly different heads and found a preference for the real faces. It is possible that these preferences are due to an initial innate interest in human faces, which would make sense. How else could an infant interact with the right class of objects unless it could recognise them in the first place? On the other hand, it is also possible that babies learn, very early on, to like faces because they are positively reinforced. Babies may initially smile at anything but only one class of objects smiles back, and this is reinforcing. Alternatively, infants may simply have a preference for symmetrical patterns. Whether or not human infants have an innate preference for faces, it is certainly true that they like looking at them.

A rather different question concerns the babies' ability to recognise a parent's face. It used to be thought that infants were unable to recognise their mothers for a few months after birth. More recent studies suggest that this ability has been hugely underestimated. Bushnell *et al.* (1989) used the PL technique, in which 2-day-old infants were given a choice between their mother's face and a stranger's. Infants looked at their mothers 63% of the time, suggesting that they were able to recognise her. Critics could argue that the baby might have been attracted by what the mother was doing or might have recognised her smell. However, Walton *et al.* (1992) tried to control for these possible sources of bias. They used the videotaped faces of 12 mothers of newborn infants which they matched with videotapes of faces of other women whose hair colour, eye colour, complexion and hair-style were the same as the mothers'. Babies of only 1 and 2 days old showed a significant preference for their mothers. This seems to suggest that babies learn very rapidly to recognise their mother's face, though this evidence is based on the assumption that longer looking time indicates preference (rather than, say, curiosity).

Depth perception

A classic early study that investigated depth perception was conducted by E.J. Gibson and R.D. Walk in 1960. They made a 'visual cliff' by placing a sheet of glass on top of a specially constructed table (see Figure 4.2). A checked pattern was positioned directly under the glass surface of one half of the table (the shallow side), but the same pattern was placed several feet below the glass surface on the other side of the table (the deep side). This arrangement gave the impression of a deep drop half-way across the table even though the glass top continued to provide a solid surface. If an infant has no depth perception, she should be happy to crawl across the whole table. If, however, a baby can judge depth, she would not want to cross over the edge of the 'cliff'.

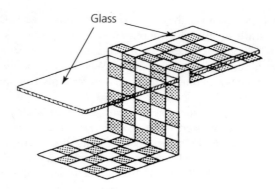

Glass

Figure 4.2 **The visual cliff test apparatus**

Gibson and Walk had to test babies who were mobile and so they were not able to use infants under the age of 6 months. They tested 36 babies between the ages of 6 and 14 months and found that most of them would crawl about on the shallow side but would not move on to the deep side even if their mothers called to them from across the other side of the deep part of the apparatus. Gibson and Walk concluded that depth perception is innate.

They later carried out the visual cliff experiment with various precocial animals (e.g. chicks, lambs, kids, etc.). If placed on the shallow side, these animals would not stray on to the deep side. If they were placed on the deep side, they either froze or refused to stand up. Rats were the only animals that would venture over the cliff, but rats rely on their whiskers as guides and touch seems to be more important to them than vision. This demonstrates how difficult it is to generalise from animal studies to human beings. However, if the whiskers were cut off, the rats were forced to rely on vision and they, too, would refuse to cross to the deep side.

These kinds of study seem to confirm that animals have innate depth perception, but it does not necessarily mean that it is innate in humans too. Remember that Gibson and Walk were using babies who were at least 6 months old so it could be argued that they had learned through experience to perceive depth.

Campos *et al.* (1970) tried to investigate this question further by using younger babies. They compared the heart rates of infants as young as 2 months old when placed on the shallow side and then on the deep side. Heart rates decreased slightly on the deep side, which suggests that the babies were able to distinguish between the two. It is interesting to note that older babies (approximately 9 months) showed an *increase* in heart rate and seemed to show more anxiety than the younger babies. One interpretation of these findings is that the perception of depth is an ability which emerges very early in life but that avoidance behaviour is only learned through experience.

Another technique used for investigating depth perception in young babies is to monitor their reaction when an object looms straight towards them. If they possess depth perception, they should react by blinking, flinching or turning their head away. Bornstein (1984) has demonstrated that babies as young as 2 months attempt some avoidance response. Studies such as these suggest that some awareness of depth perception occurs in very young human babies.

Constancies

We discussed constancies in Chapter 3, so you will understand how important they are for making sense of our visual environment. The intriguing question for psychologists is whether these constancies are innate or learned. Size and shape constancy are the ones that have been investigated the most so we shall look at evidence related to them.

Size constancy

A classic experiment was conducted by Bower in 1966. He showed infants aged between 6 and 12 weeks a 30 cm. cube at a distance of 1 metre. He trained them through a process of conditioning (see Table 4.1) to turn their heads whenever they were presented with this cube. Each time they turned their head, they were rewarded by an adult popping up, smiling at them and tickling them. This peekaboo game seemed to act as a powerful reward for the babies and they quickly learned to turn their heads in response to the 30 cm. cube. Once they had learned this response, Bower introduced three different cube presentations:

1. A *30 cm.* cube positioned *3 metres* away.
2. A *90 cm.* cube positioned *3 metres* away.
3. A *90 cm.* cube positioned *1 metre* away.

Think about this in terms of what you read in Chapter 3. If the infants had size constancy they would look at Stimulus 1 (i.e. the original cube further away) and recognise it as the same and turn their heads for a reward. Stimulus 2, although a much larger cube, would throw the same retinal image as the original cube because, although it is three times larger, it is also three times further away. Stimulus 3 consisted of a larger cube but at the same distance as the original (i.e. retinal image would be greater).

Bower found that infants turned their heads 58 times to Stimulus 1, 54 times to Stimulus 3 but only 22 times to Stimulus 2 where both object size and distance were different from the original. He concluded that babies have innate size constancy.

Later studies have not found such convincing evidence for size constancy in very young babies (McKenzie *et al.*,1980). However, it seems likely that infants at 6 months, with their increased under-standing of depth perception, have acquired some aspects of size constancy.

Shape constancy

Shape constancy, too, is important for the baby so that he or she realises that a cup or a toy is still the same, even when it is viewed from a different angle. Bower, again using a conditioning technique, found that 2-month-old babies responded to a tilted rectangle as if it were the original rectangle. Later studies suggest (Bornstein *et al.*, 1986) that this ability to maintain shape constancy emerges slightly later at about 3 to 4 months.

As you can see, the human infant seems to be born with quite a wide range of perceptual abilities. Some of these abilities develop as the visual system matures, but others probably improve as a result of learning and interacting with the visual environment.

Evidence from non-human animal studies

Most investigations using animals have taken the form of visual deprivation studies. If perceptual abilities are innate, then deprivation should have no effect and animals restored to a normal environment should be able to perceive normally again. If, however, perceptual abilities are learned, then deprivation will have a marked effect.

Riesen (1947) was one of the first people to try and investigate this question. He reared chimps in total darkness until they were 16 months old. The only light exposure was a brief period during feeding times. The chimps did not show normal perceptual abilities. For example, they did not blink when objects were moved suddenly towards their faces and seemed not to recognize objects in their environment unless they accidentally touched them.

Weiskrantz (1956) showed that light is needed for the cells in the retina to develop properly. Animals reared in total darkness do not appear to have a fully developed visual system. Maturational processes appear to need visual stimulation from the environment in order to develop normally.

Riesen (1965) experimented further and reared a chimp in translucent goggles which allowed diffuse and unpatterned light into the eye for one and a half hours a day. For the rest of the day, the chimp was left in darkness. This animal showed markedly inferior perceptual abilities when compared to chimps reared in normal conditions. For example, she was very slow to follow moving objects with her eyes and she seemed to have difficulty in recognizing objects. Riesen concluded from this, and other studies with monkeys and kittens, that light is necessary for the development of perceptual abilities.

Hubel (1977) reported that the visual cortex does not develop normally in monkeys that have one eye sewn shut for the first 18 months of life. Specifically, he found that groups of cells in the visual cortex which responded to the open eye had expanded, while groups dealing with input from the closed eye had diminished.

Blakemore and Cooper (1970) reared kittens in the dark and exposed them to an environment that had only vertical lines for five hours each day. The kittens wore ruffs round their necks to prevent them from tilting their heads to turn the vertical lines into horizontal. After five months of this selective rearing, they showed visual impairment and did not respond to horizontal lines at all; for instance, they tripped over horizontal wires. Even after prolonged exposure to a normal environment, they remained unresponsive to horizontal lines. This does not mean that horizontal line recognition is learned however. Blakemore and Cooper found that many cells in the visual cortex of these kittens responded to vertical lines but none of them responded to horizontal lines. It seems likely, then, that cells responsive to horizontal lines are present at birth but, if not stimulated in the first few months (i.e. by being raised in an exclusively vertical world), they are taken over by competing systems.

Held and Hein (1963) were interested in the relationship between perception and movement. They used the apparatus below to investigate this relationship. Kittens reared in the dark spent three hours a day in the apparatus. One kitten (the active kitten) could move around the apparatus though this movement was limited to a fixed circuit. Its movements were transmitted to a passive kitten (i.e. strapped into an apparatus preventing independent movement). Every time the active kitten moved, the passive kitten would be pulled at the same speed and cover the same distance. After ten days' exposure to this treatment, the active kitten was normal in terms of perception but the passive kitten lacked certain abilities and did not show stress when placed on the deep side of the visual cliff (see Figure, 4.2). However, when allowed to move around freely in a normal environment, the passive kitten soon acquired this response. This suggests that the kittens were not able to learn appropriate

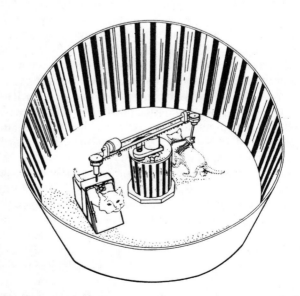

Figure 4.3 The 'kitten carousel' apparatus (adapted from Held and Hein, 1963)

motor responses because of their restricted upbringing, and this experiment shows that perception relied on learning perceptual motor coordination. (This experiment is described in more detail on p. 117.)

Evaluation

The basic argument that deprivation should have no effect on innate abilities is too simplistic because perceptual abilities may be present at birth but deteriorate due to a lack of crucial environmental stimulation at a critical early developmental period.

The study of non-human animals raises some important issues. Perception is a complex process and we should be cautious before we generalise the results of animal studies to human perception. Visuo-motor co-ordination can show a temporary deficit which can be remedied if the animal is restored to a normal environment, but some perceptual deficits are permanent and never restored (e.g. blindness to horizontal lines).

What is clear is that normal development of the visual system depends on light stimulation. This may involve maturational processes (biological development under genetic control) and there may be sensitive periods when the animal is maximally responsive to stimulation from the environment.

Another key issue is an ethical one concerning the use of animals in experiments. Many of these studies were carried out a long time ago in a different ethical climate and most would be considered as unethical projects today, for instance, the distress caused to experimental participants.

1. Identify the main findings from the study of animals discussed above.
2. Write a paragraph summarising the key criticisms of work in this area.

Progress exercise

Evidence from cataract studies

An interesting source of information on the nature/nurture debate comes from the study of people with damaged visual systems. Various optical disorders have been investigated (e.g. astigmatism, a curvature of the lens which produces distorted vision) but we shall focus on studies of cataract patients (also discussed on p. 76).

One of the best known case studies was reported by Gregory and Wallace (1963). A man, referred to as S.B., had been blind since birth until a corneal graft operation restored his sight at the age of 52. He was able to focus on objects and to track moving objects that he already knew through touch but, for objects or features where touch had not been available, he usually required a long, slow learning process. Perhaps, surprisingly, he was immediately able to tell the time visually. This was thought to be because he had years of experience of feeling the hands of the pocket watch he kept on him. As a boy at a school for the blind, he had been taught to recognise capital letters by touching their outlines on especially embossed plates. This was designed to help the children recognise street signs when they were out. S.B. was immediately able to read capital letters, but it took him a long time to learn to recognise lower case letters.

Although S.B. had the immediate ability to recognise certain things, he never became perceptually normal. He was able to transfer knowledge from touch to vision but had enormous difficulties in recognising things he had not experienced through touch. For example, he had no experience of shadows and would often stumble on steps because he tried to stand on the shadow. When shown a picture of the Necker Cube, S.B. did not experience reversals (see p. 27) and saw it as flat. He was able to judge horizontal distances well (e.g. how far he was standing from a chair) but was puzzled by vertical distance. Shortly after surgery, while still in hospital, he thought that the pavement outside was within touching distance whereas, in reality, his room was several storeys above ground level. He also had difficulty judging the speed of oncoming traffic when crossing the road.

This was a fascinating study and gave psychologists the opportunity to see the effects of long-term visual deprivation in a human being. However, it is difficult to draw any firm conclusions about the development of perception from this and other studies of visually impaired adults. S.B. was not like a new-born baby learning to see, because he already had a huge store of knowledge gained through touch and this assisted him in interpreting novel visual stimuli. He continued to prefer touch to vision and often, with his eyes shut, would touch unfamiliar objects; only then could he see them when he opened his eyes.

Sadly, like many other people reported in cataract cases, S.B. became severely depressed because he found his new visual world ugly and confusing.

Evidence from readjustment studies

George Stratton (1896) was the first person to report on readjustment studies. He reasoned that, if certain aspects of perception were learned, it ought to be feasible to acquire a new set of percepts. He blindfolded one of his eyes and strapped a device to the other one which rotated the field of view through 180° (i.e. it turned his world upside-down). Stratton kept a diary which, although difficult to interpret, suggests that adaptation did take place. However, it seemed that he only adapted his motor responses in order to deal with this upside-down world and did not actually see the world differently. The world did not appear to be the right way up when he was wearing the device and he did not experience any problems when he removed it after eight days.

Kohler (1962) asked observers to wear similar optically distorting devices for several weeks. For the first few days, the observers experienced the world as being very unstable. They had difficulty in walking and needed assistance to perform quite simple tasks. However, after only a few days, they had adapted well and one observer was even able to ride a bike. Kohler believed that a real perceptual change had occurred because, once the distorting lenses were removed, observers experienced some disorientation and they again had some difficulties moving about. However, these so-called after-effects disappeared very quickly and, within an hour, they had completely readapted to the normal world.

Harris (1980) used prisms which cause a rather less dramatic change of visual input. When viewing an object through the prisms, it appears to have shifted to one side. When observers reached for an object, they tended to miss it at first because they reached to the side. They learned fairly quickly to adjust so that they could locate the object accurately but, after the prisms were removed, they experienced after-effects so that, back in the undistorted world, they now missed objects they reached for because they were continuing to make the adjustment. However, as with Kohler's participants, the after-effects soon disappeared. Hess (1950) conducted a similar study with chickens which failed to adapt when pecking for food. This suggests that non-human animal perception is quite different and perhaps less adaptable.

Evaluation

These studies suggest that any genuine perceptual learning which had occurred during the readjustment period was pretty fragile. However, it does seem that human adults are able to adapt to a new environment, and so it seems that learning plays an important role.

Held and Bossom (1961) were interested in finding out what conditions are necessary for perceptual readjustment to occur. They placed human participants in an apparatus similar to the kitten carousel (see p. 86). Active observers wearing distorting goggles walked around in the apparatus for an hour while passive observers were pushed around the same path in a wheelchair for the same amount of time. At the end of an hour, perceptual adaptation had occurred in the active observers but not in the passive observers. This suggests that adaptation depends on active movement. In fact, it may be the case that people in a visually distorted world do not actually learn to *perceive* it normally but simply *adopt the appropriate motor behaviour* to allow them to cope safely and efficiently with this strange environment.

Evidence from cross-cultural studies

A number of studies have been conducted with different cultural groups and most of these have used visual illusions. The aim of such studies is to find out whether people brought up outside a Western culture experience illusions in the same way. If it can be demonstrated that cultural groups differ in their interpretation of such stimuli, it can be reasonably assumed that environmental factors play an important role in perception. The findings from these studies generally do support the role of learning in perception but it is not always easy to draw appropriate conclusions from them. Cross-cultural studies will be discussed in more detail in Chapter 5.

Conclusions

It is clear from the evidence presented in this chapter that some perceptual abilities are innate and others develop later. There is no evidence to support either of the extreme views that perception is either wholly learned or wholly innate. The nature/nurture problem is really one of understanding the complex interaction between the expression of genetic factors and the influence of the environment.

Summary

The nature/nurture debate has dominated the study of perceptual development. There are several ways to study the problem. The most direct way is to study human neonates but there are problems associated with this kind of research. On the whole, evidence from this type of research gives some support to the nativist position. Animal experiments have shown that an ordinary, visual environment is needed for normal perceptual development, and restored vision studies of human beings support this. Distorted worlds and readjustment studies indicate that human perceptual systems are flexible but the learning of new motor movements is part of the adaptation. Cross-cultural studies show contradictory results, but some differences in susceptibility to illusions have been demonstrated, which supports the empiricist position. Psychologists are now in agreement that there is no clear-cut answer to the problem and an interactionist viewpoint is the best approach.

Complete the following table for all the methods in the study of the development of visual perception.

Method of study	Main advantages	Main disadvatanges	Example of research using this method
Neonate studies etc.			

Further reading

Davenport, G.C. (1994) *An Introduction to Child Development*, 2nd edn, London: Collins Educational. Chapter 13 covers issues raised in this chapter in an easy to read style with good illustrations.

Hayes, N. (1993) *A First Course in Psychology*, 3rd edn, Walton-on-Thames: Thomas Nelson & Sons. Contains a very good general account of key studies in the area of perceptual development and is very easy to read.

Smith, P.K. (1992) *Understanding Children's Development*, 2nd edn, Oxford: Blackwell. Contains a chapter with a very readable account of human neonate studies. It is particularly interesting on face recognition.

5

Individual, social and cultural variations in perceptual organisation

Introduction
Individual and psychological variations
Cultural and social variations
Summary

Introduction

In the previous chapters, we have looked at perception as though everyone experiences it in the same way. In Chapter 4 we showed how perception is a developmental process which matures with age and experience, but the emphasis was still on shared patterns of development and on the fact that similar sequences are seen in *all* infants. We now need to consider whether *individuals* differ from one another in the way they experience their perceptual worlds. Given that perception is ultimately an *interpretation* of incoming sensory stimuli, it seems likely that individuals might experience rather different perceptions when encountering identical stimuli.

There are probably several factors which give rise to different perceptual experiences:

- *Individual and psychological* (e.g. age, gender, personality, physiological state, mood, individual life-experience).
- *Social and cultural* (e.g. environmental conditions: weather, geography, etc., the company we keep, cultural background and tradition).

In this chapter, we will consider some of these factors.

Individual and psychological variations

Age

We have already seen (Chapter 4) that perceptual abilities change and mature as the human infant develops. These are individual differences in so far as they are differences which vary between older and younger individuals or in the same people as they age. In general, perceptual abilities seem to improve and allow an increasingly accurate representation of the physical world, but there are certain perceptual abilities which seem to deteriorate with age. For example, thickening of the lens (see Chapter 1) with age can affect colour perception (particularly blue/green and white/yellow distinctions) and, together with reduced pupil size in the ageing eye, limits the amount of light reaching the retina and so reduces sensitivity (Corso, 1981).

There is also substantial age-related loss of neurons in the visual cortex which can cause a reduction in visual acuity (Weale, 1986). Many of these changes occur gradually and can be almost imperceptible to the individual concerned, but they can bring about considerable differences in his/her perception of the world.

Gender

The issue of gender differences in psychological processes is controversial. Several gender differences have been clearly demonstrated in the perception of touch, taste and smell but, for visual perception, the picture is not so clear-cut. However, there seem to be some broad differences between males and females in visual perception. Males appear to have better visual acuity in daylight conditions whereas females seem to dark-adapt more quickly than males (McGuinness, 1976). There is also some evidence that levels of visual acuity vary in women across their menstrual cycle (Parlee, 1983).

One ability which seems to produce fairly consistent sex differences is performance on visual-spatial tasks. Examples of visual-spatial tasks are: visualising how objects will appear when they are rotated; detecting the orientations of, and relationships between, different stimuli; and accurately perceiving complex visual patterns. Males generally seem to be better at such tasks than females (Halpern, 1986).

Personality

People with different personalities tend to behave differently in various social situations and may respond differently to information of various sorts. Psychologists have raised the question whether personality can also affect the way people perceive the world (see Figure 5.1). This is an example of an embedded figures test and has been used to distinguish between individuals in terms of their personality (Ward, 1985). People who have difficulty in detecting a target in a complex figure are called 'field dependent' (Witkin *et al.*, 1962). They are characterised as being socially dependent, conforming, sensitive to their social surroundings and keen to make a good impression. Individuals who experience little difficulty with disembedding the target figure are called 'field independent' and are described, in personality terms, as self-reliant, inner directed and individualistic. The classifications of 'field dependent' and 'field independent' map loosely on to the personality classifications of Eysenck (1967) (namely **extrovert** and **introvert**). Several studies have investigated the effect of introversion-extroversion on perception. For example, introverts have more sensitive visual perception and are better at perceptual tasks requiring sustained attention (Harkins and Green, 1975).

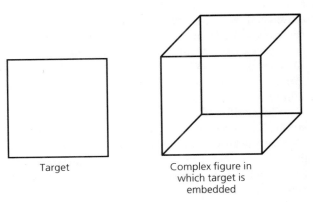

Target

Complex figure in
which target is
embedded

Figure 5.1 **An embedded figures test**

Kagan (1971) has been particularly interested in differences between children and he identified a personality dimension he called 'conceptual tempo'. He measured the speed and attention with which children look at objects and situations and found that some children (reflective) adopt a slower tempo, whereas others (impulsive) are much faster. In a longitudinal study, Kagan *et al.* (1978) found that infants designated as either reflective or impulsive would still be classified in the same way at the age of 10, suggesting that this might be a fairly stable characteristic. Reflective children tend to look at things for longer and examine them in closer detail. Impulsive children scan scenes more quickly and do not dwell on detail. Reflective skills are extremely helpful for many tasks at school, especially in the early stages of learning to read, and reflective children have been found to do somewhat better academically than impulsive children (Haskins and McKinney, 1976).

Physiological states

There are many types of physical damage that can cause disruption to visual perception. We have already considered the effects of cataract removal in Chapter 4, but there are other sorts of injury or disease which can give rise to perceptual difficulties as well. A particular kind of problem, called an **agnosia**, occurs when individuals appear to see accurately but cannot make sense of the information in the visual stimulus. Object agnosia refers to the inability to name, recognise or use objects accurately and is believed to be due to lesions in the secondary visual areas of the cortex. Luria (1973) described a patient who was given a picture of a pair of glasses to identify. The patient examined the picture carefully, and was eventually able to decipher two circles and some kind of bar linking them. He tried to make sense of this by suggesting, wrongly, that it was a picture of a bicycle.

People suffering from a very rare disorder called **prosopagnosia** are unable to recognise human faces and may not even be able to identify their own face in a mirror. This disorder has interested psychologists because it helps them to understand more about face recognition which seems to be such an important part of human perception (see Chapter 4).

All the agnosias appear to be caused by damage to particular brain sites, usually in the secondary or even tertiary visual processing areas rather than in the primary visual cortex. They are fairly rare disorders which bring about bizarre and unusual changes to perception. They are of interest to psychologists because they provide insights into the location of some of our perceptual capacities in the brain.

The kind of altered physical states we discussed above occur through accidental damage or disease. Sometimes we alter our physiological state deliberately through the ingestion of certain substances. Substances like drugs can significantly alter human perception. Hallucinogenic and psychoactive drugs like LSD and marijuana are known to produce detrimental effects to the visual system even though users often claim enhanced visual clarity and acuity. Colour discrimination is impaired (Hartman and Hollister, 1963) and vision becomes blurred (Hoffer and Osmond, 1967). There is also evidence of changes in depth perception and distortions in perception of size (Tart, 1971).

The drugs mentioned so far are illegal substances, but many drugs in common use can also alter perception, for example, stimulants like caffeine and depressants like alcohol and tobacco. Alcohol can affect the ability to follow a moving target with the eyes (Levy *et al.*, 1981) and decreases the ability to change the focus of the lens (Miller *et al.*, 1985). Similarly, smoking produces alterations in certain visual tasks, particularly those involving sustained attention (Gliner *et al.*, 1983). It also affects night vision, which could account for the fact that smokers tend to have more night-time driving accidents than non-smokers (Rhee *et al.*, 1965).

Even common medicines like aspirin and antihistamines can cause dimness and blurring of vision while everyday stimulants such as caffeine actually seem to enhance visual acuity. Thus someone who has just drunk a cup of coffee or a glass of wine or taken a painkiller for a headache may temporarily differ from other individuals in terms of perceptual experience.

Perceptual set

Set refers to the expectancies or predispositions which an observer brings to a perceptual situation. Our background and experience seem to 'programme' us to 'see' situations in a particular way, especially in conditions where the stimulus input is degraded or ambiguous. There are several factors which seem to influence set, and they include context, expectations, motivation, past experience and emotion. These factors often interact to produce perceptual set.

One classic experiment to demonstrate the effects of set was carried out by Bruner and Postman (1949). They showed observers playing cards on a screen for a brief period of time. The playing cards were unusual in that hearts and diamonds were coloured black and spades and clubs were coloured red. After brief exposures, observers reported that the cards were normal, presumably because experience with playing cards led them to *expect* the normal colours. When the observers were exposed to the cards for a slightly longer time, they realised that something was wrong but, because their expectations about cards were so deep-rooted, they suggested compromise explanations for what they had seen. For example, some people said that they had seen brown or purple hearts and others believed that they had seen black shapes with red edges. This is interesting, because it suggests that previous experience can outweigh the evidence of our own eyes and produce a genuine perceptual distortion (see Chapter 3 for an explanation of visual illusions).

Expectancy is probably the reason why we often fail to notice misprints. Have you ever handed in one of your essays, confident that you have checked it for errors, and received it back from the teacher with a couple of spelling errors and, perhaps, a missing word pointed out? You probably do not notice these errors yourself because you are expecting to see the correct word and so 'read' it as correct even if it is not. Consider the example 'Paris in the the spring'. Even professional proofreaders sometimes fall into this trap, which is the reason why books and newspapers contain occasional misprints.

Occupational background can also be a factor in determining set. Toch and Schulte (1961) conducted an interesting study into the perception of violence and crime. They compared the performance of a group of advanced police students with a group of new police students and a group of university students. They used a piece of equipment called a stereoscope to present a different picture simultaneously to each eye. One picture showed a violent scene (e.g. a man with a gun standing over a body) and the other showed a non-violent scene (e.g. a man mowing the lawn). Observers who are shown two different pictures in a stereoscope usually resolve the perceptual confusion by selecting one scene in preference to the other and this scene then dominates the perception. They found that the advanced police students were twice as likely to favour the violent scene than the other two groups. This suggests that the occupational training they had received predisposed them to look out for wrongdoing. Of course, it is not only policemen whose perception is affected by set. For example, imagine an insurance agent and an interior designer coming to your home – they are likely to notice very different things.

One aspect of perception related to the concept of set is **perceptual defence**. This was a term coined by McGinnies (1949). He demonstrated that observers took longer to respond to sexual and taboo words than to neutral words presented on a screen. These findings seem to demonstrate that things which evoke unpleasant emotions take longer to be recognised at a conscious level. However, one obvious criticism is that people are too embarrassed to report taboo words and this explains the delayed response times.

Give a brief summary of the individual and psychological factors which influence perception.

Progress exercise

Cultural and social variations

It seems that there are aspects of our environmental and cultural background that equip us with different perceptual strategies and may lead us to experience the world in different ways. So, for example, people who live in dense, tropical forests are never exposed to the kind of broad, panoramic vistas experienced by desert tribes. People who have been brought up in Western cultures take for granted certain visual stimuli (e.g. photos, film and television), but these could be puzzling to someone brought up in a pre-literate tribal group. These kinds of differences in background, particularly when experienced over a lifetime, are likely to lead to different perceptual experiences.

Many of the studies concerned with cultural variations in perception have concentrated on the experience of visual illusions. In a classic study, Segall *et al.* (1963) compared the responsiveness of different cultural groups to the Müller-Lyer and the horizontal-vertical illusions. They tested people from various parts of Africa and also the Philippines with people from Illinois in the United States. They believed that people brought up in the urbanised West, where rooms and buildings are usually rectangular, would be more susceptible to these illusions than people brought up in more open and less carpentered environments (see Chapter 3 for an explanation of visual illusions). Although there were some variations *within* the non-carpentered groups, on average the Müller-Lyer illusion was greater for the Westerners than for the others (see p. 58 for another example of a cross-cultural study).

The findings were not so clear-cut for the horizontal-vertical illusion. Two of the African tribes in the study lived in very open country with vast, uninterrupted views. For them, vertical markers in the landscape (e.g. trees) were important for estimating distance. These two tribes were particularly susceptible to the horizontal-vertical illusion – in fact, they experienced it to a greater extent than the Westerners. Members of another African tribe, however, who lived in a dense jungle environment where vistas extended, at the most, for only about 30 m., were the least likely of all the groups studied to see the illusion.

Similar results have been reported for other perspective-related illusions (e.g. Coren and Girgus, 1978). These findings lend powerful support to the idea that our physical environment can affect our perceptual experience.

Carpentered world explanations

Not all psychologists would agree with the conclusions of Segall *et al.* that the differences reported reflect the carpentered environment (see the key study on p. 118). Gregor and McPherson (1965) found no differences in susceptibility to illusions between two groups of Australian aborigines, even though one group lived in an urban, carpentered environment and the other lived a more traditional, outdoor life. Jahoda (1966) looked at two Ghanaian tribes who differed in their environments. The carpentered world hypothesis would predict that the tribe living on plains in round huts would be more susceptible to the horizontal-vertical illusion and less susceptible to the Müller-Lyer illusion than the tribe living in rectangular huts in dense forest.

Jahoda found no such differences and so cast some doubt on the interpretations of the Segall *et al.* environment. He believed that certain other cultural variables, which had been ignored in Segall's study, might account for the different experiences of visual illusions. In particular, Jahoda felt that non-Western groups might find it difficult to understand two-dimensional drawings of three-dimensional objects. In Western cultures we are exposed to drawings and photos from a very early age and have no difficulty in interpreting them but, if you think about it, there are many differences between pictures and real images (size, flatness, colour, etc.). When we look at pictures, we have to be able to identify objects *and* interpret the three-dimensional arrangement implied in the flat image. It is possible that people from other cultural backgrounds may have problems with either or both of these aspects of interpretation.

Deprivation studies

Hochberg and Brooks (1962) conducted a rather unusual study on one of their own children. The boy was raised until the age of 19 months without being exposed to any pictorial representation. He was shielded from books, magazines and newspapers and was not allowed to watch television. His parents even removed pictures from food tins and packets. At the end of this period, the child was perfectly capable of identifying pictures of common items even though he had no previous exposure to pictures. Although we cannot draw firm conclusions from a case study like this (and we cannot be sure that the child had been completely isolated), it suggests that we do not have to learn to interpret drawings as real-world objects. It is important to also question the ethics of this study.

Two-dimensional drawings

Deregowski (1980) has reported on a number of instances where pictures have been presented to people reared in isolated cultures with no exposure to two-dimensional drawings. These are largely anecdotal reports from missionaries and health workers rather than well-controlled studies, but they offer some interesting insights. One report from a missionary in Malawi suggests that, after initial puzzlement, individuals could identify objects from drawings. Having shown them a black and white drawing of an ox and a dog, he writes:

> If there are few boys about, you say: 'This really is a picture of an ox and a dog. Look at the horn of the ox, and there is his tail.' And the boy will say: 'Oh! Yes and there is the dog's nose and eyes and ears!' Then the old people will look again and clasp their hands and say, 'Oh! Yes, it is a dog.'

This kind of anecdotal evidence suggests that, although object identification from pictures is not necessarily spontaneous, it quickly occurs when attention is appropriately directed.

Another report came from a health worker who showed pictures on a screen to a group of Africans:

> When all the people were quickly seated, the first picture flashed on the sheet was that of an elephant. The wildest excitement immediately prevailed, many of the people jumping up and shouting, fearing the beast must be alive, whilst those nearest to the sheet sprang up and fled.

This suggests that object identification in this case was instantaneous and vivid, even though there was no understanding of the artificiality of the picture.

It seems, then, that object identification is either instantly possible or quickly acquired. However, it may be more difficult for people from non-Western cultures to understand the implied spatial relationships in pictures. In order to perceive depth in a flat image, we have to take account of certain depth cues which might be included in the drawing or photo. Many pictures contain depth cues such as linear perspective, texture gradient, overlap, height in the visual plane, etc. (see Chapter 3). However, other cues are absent from flat pictures, so, for example, there is no retinal disparity between items in the picture and all the elements require the same amount of accommodation and convergence (see Chapter 3). Pictures, by their static nature, are also unable to show motion parallax. Pick (1987) suggests that in order to see a drawing as representing an array of objects in three dimensions instead of as a flat surface with different light and dark shadings, we have to attend to some depth cues and ignore the absence of others. It could be that people who have no familiarity with pictures find it difficult to use pictorial cues in this way.

Hudson (1960) investigated this possibility by showing different groups of people a series of line drawings that made use of various pictorial depth cues. An example of one of his pictures is given in Figure 5.2. As you can see, this picture includes the depth cues of familiar size, overlap and height in the visual plane and you will have no difficulty in interpreting it as a hunter trying to spear an antelope with an elephant in the distance. Hudson's series of pictures have been used with people from a variety of African tribes and the results seem quite clear.

Deregowski (1980) has reported on a number of studies and concluded that adults and children alike found it fairly easy to identify the objects in the pictures but much more difficult to perceive depth. A common misinterpretation was that the hunter was trying to

Figure 5.2 **A drawing used by Hudson (1960). Reprinted with permission of the Helen Dwight Reid Educational Foundation. Published by Heldref Publications, 1319 18th Street, NW, Washington, DC 20036-1802**

spear the elephant. This showed that the observers had not responded to any of the cues which placed the elephant at a greater distance from the hunter than the antelope. By the same token we might misinterpret drawings of, say, cave paintings because we apply Western depth cues that were not intended by the artist.

It has been shown that the ability to perceive three-dimensionality in pictures improves with formal education which includes the use of picture books and other pictorial stimuli (Pick, 1987). Interestingly, it also seems to improve when additional depth cues such as texture gradient and aerial perspective are included in the picture (Hagen and Jones, 1978). So, it seems that it is wrong to conclude that non-Western, non-urbanised cultures can never understand pictorial cues. It is likely that some cues such as texture gradient are more apparent to them than others such as familiar size.

One pictorial convention that is rarely understood by non-Westernised cultures is the cartoonist's trick of implying motion. Think of the way in which cartoonists can imply with a few strokes of the pen that a dog's tail is wagging or a car is speeding along the road. There is, of course, no actual motion but we infer motion from the picture, and there is evidence that this ability appears as early as 4 years of age in Western cultures (Friedman and Stevenson, 1975). In non-Western cultures with no experience of such cartoon pictures, motion is rarely seen. Duncan *et al.* (1973) showed cartoon pictures to a group of rural African children of a boy whose head was drawn in three different positions to imply rapid turning of his head. The children showed no understanding of implied movement and half of them reported that they thought the boy was deformed! However, Duncan *et al.* found, in comparison studies, that factors such as education, urbanisation and exposure to pictures all increased the likelihood that movement would be seen.

Assessment of cross-cultural studies

Cross-cultural studies have yielded some interesting findings but, as you can see, they are often beset by methodological problems (such as observer bias and poor sampling methods) and can be difficult to interpret. Some of the conclusions are based on anecdotal reports rather than controlled experiments and even some of the systematic studies have not controlled for possible confounding variables.

It is possible that some perceptual abilities have been underestimated because of the techniques used. Deregowski (1972) studied the Me'en tribe of Ethiopia who lived in a fairly isolated area cut off from Western influence. When Deregowski showed them drawings of animals, they responded by feeling, smelling and even tasting the paper but showed no interest in or recognition of the pictures.

Had the study finished there, it would have been easy to conclude that the Me'en people had no understanding of pictorial material. In fact, Deregowski continued the study by presenting them with a new set of pictures. However, this time the pictures were enlarged (i.e. slightly more realistic) and painted on cloth (a familiar material). These pictures were easily recognised by most of the tribespeople. This example illustrates how important it is not to draw premature conclusions.

It is possible that people from different cultures have problems with Western-style pictorial art on aesthetic grounds and that they prefer a more familiar style of art. Hudson (reported in Deregowski, 1972) found that Africans with little exposure to Western culture prefer split drawings to the kind of perspective drawings generally preferred by Westerners. See Figure 5.3.

Deregowski believes that children from all cultures have a preference for split drawings and that young children show this preference in their own drawing even in cultures where the style is considered wrong by adults. According to Deregowski, most societies suppress this preference because the resulting drawings do not convey information as accurately as perspective drawings (for example, an architect's drawing of a house could not use the split style). However, some societies have developed split drawing to a high artistic level, particularly where the drawings are regarded as decorative or symbolic rather than as a means of conveying information about objects.

The key problem is the meaning of realism in art. Photos and pictures do not necessarily capture what the eye really sees. Abstract artists convey meaning and communicate through a medium of shared experience between the artist and the observers. The ancient Egyptians, for example, drew not what they could see but what they knew to be the most important or characteristic aspects of the figure. People, for example, were drawn with heads in profile and arms and legs from the side, but with eyes, shoulders and chest drawn in

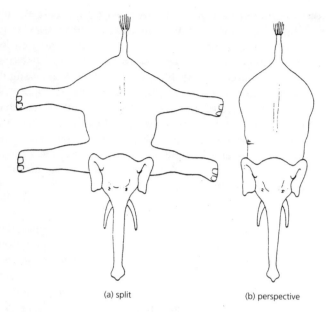

(a) split   (b) perspective

Figure 5.3 **Split and perspective drawings of an elephant**

full-face view. The important thing was that the image was drawn as the artist knew it to be rather than that it should represent an accurate version of reality.

Perception, seeing and knowing interact in complex ways. Cultural effects on behaviour are complex and little understood. Much more research needs to be carried out if psychologists are going to unravel and understand the role that an individual's culture has in the experience of visual perception. The research might have some useful applications as well, such as the education of ethnically mixed groups.

Summary

Perception is a highly complex activity which seems to depend on several levels of processing. Although there are many broad similarities in the way people process perceptual information and in the way they develop their perceptual abilities, it seems likely, given the variations in education, life experience, cultural background, expectations and temperament, that individuals might differ slightly in their perception of the world. We have looked at several factors such as age, gender, personality, physiological state and experience that might cause individuals to have different perceptions of the same visual stimuli. We have also considered studies that have investigated the effects of culture and environment on perception. Some of the evidence from such studies is contradictory and difficult to interpret, but it does seem clear that perception does not occur in exactly the same way for everyone. Perception is in the eye of the beholder.

1. Describe and evaluate some key studies carried out in the investigation of cultural differences and similarities in perception. Use the table below to help you do this.

Review exercise

Description of study	Main findings	Evaluation

2. Write a brief account summarising the main problems encountered by researchers in the study of cross-cultural comparisons in perception.

Further reading

Berry, J.B., Poortinga, Y.H., Segall, M.H. and Dasen, P.R. (eds) (1992) *Cross-cultural Psychology: Research and Applications*, New York: Cambridge University Press. Chapter 6 covers many issues raised by this chapter. Although a more advanced text it is detailed and fairly easy to read.

Matsumoto, D. (1994) *People: Psychology from a Cultural Perspective*, Pacific Grove, California: Brookes/Cole. Chapter 3 deals with perception and provides a good basic introduction to key issues.

Serpell, R. (1976) *Culture's Influence on Behaviour*, *Essential Psychology*, ed. P. Herriot, London: Methuen & Co. Ltd. Although written a long time ago this text is concise yet very detailed and covers much of the early work in this area.

6

Study aids

IMPROVING YOUR ESSAY WRITING SKILLS

At this point in the book you have acquired the knowledge necessary to tackle the exam yourself. Answering exam questions is a skill, and in this chapter we hope to help you improve this skill. A common mistake that some students make is not providing the kind of evidence the examiner is looking for. Another is failing to properly answer the question, despite providing lots of information. Typically, a grade C answer is accurate and reasonably constructed, but has limited detail and commentary. To lift such an answer to an A or B grade may require no more than fuller detail, better use of material and coherent organisation. By studying the essays below, and the comments that follow, you can learn how to turn your grade C answers into grade A. Please note that marks given by the examiner in the practice essays should be used as a guide only and are not definitive. They represent the 'raw marks' given by an AEB examiner; that is, the marks the examiner would give to the examining board based on a total of 24 marks per question broken down into Skill A (description) and Skill B (evaluation). A table showing this scheme is in Appendix C of Paul Humphreys' series title, *Exam Success in AEB Psychology*. They may not be the marks given on the examination certificate received ultimately by the student because all examining boards are required to use a common standardised system called the Uniform Mark Scale (UMS) which adjusts all raw scores to a single standard acceptable to all examining boards.

The essays are about the length a student would be able to write in 35–40 minutes (leaving you extra time for planning and checking). Each essay is followed by detailed comments about its strengths and weaknesses. The most common problems to look out for are:

- Students frequently fail to answer the actual question set, and present 'one they made earlier' (the Blue Peter answer).
- Many weak essays suffer from a lack of evaluation or commentary.
- On the other hand, sometimes students go too far in the other direction and their essays are all evaluation. Description is vital in demonstrating your knowledge and understanding of the selected topic.
- Don't write 'everything you know' in the hope that something will get credit. Excellence is displayed through selectivity and therefore improvements can often be made by *removing* material which is irrelevant to the question set.

For more ideas on how to write good essays you should consult *Exam Success in AEB Psychology* (in this series) by Paul Humphreys.

Practice essay 1

(a) **Outline some findings from research studies in the area of perceptual development. (6 marks)**

(b) **Describe and assess methods used in the study of perceptual development (18 marks).**

AEB 1997 Summer

Starting point: This essay was written by a candidate under examination conditions and reflects a typical answer to questions in this area.

*In this essay part (a) is asking for an **outline** of the **findings** of **some** studies. Outline means give a summary description in brief form. Answers could be general and include a number of studies, or be more specific and discuss two or three. The answer can be totally descriptive but the term **development** is crucial.*

*Part (b) requires you to both describe and assess but is asking specifically for you to focus on the **methods** used by psychologists to study perceptual development.*

(a) The area of perceptual development centres around the nature/ nurture debate. Nativists believe that perception is innate while empiricists believe that perception is learned and affected by the environment. There are many studies which support both sides.

Gibson's visual cliff results remained inconclusive about human perception as the babies used were 6 weeks old and so had six weeks of visual experience, 92% of children failed to cross [the glass]. Animals with whiskers felt the glass and so walked across. This experiment suggests that perception is innate. Fantz's experiments found that young babies had innate perception, and they preferred to look at complex patterns rather than plain ones. Both these experiments suggest that perception is innate.

The nature studies are deprivation studies. Blakemore and Cooper carried out a deprivation study on kittens and it was found out in this experiment that in kittens perception is learned. Lack of stimulation from the environment caused perceptual deficiencies in kittens. Held and Hein carried out another deprivation study on kittens. In this experiment it was found that physical experience is as important as visual experience when perception is involved. This study again suggested that perception is learned. A cross-cultural study carried out by Turnbull also suggests that perception is learned. These studies suggest that we are born with considerable perceptual abilities which are then shaped and formed by the environment around us.

1. The candidate has chosen to approach the question from the nature/nurture perspective which is fine as it is made relevant to the question. Since the question requires an 'outline' of the studies, breadth is more important than detail. The candidate has named and outlined five studies and given sufficient detail of each. Therefore 6 out of 6 marks are approriate for this part of the essay. It is better than 'slightly limited' given the mark allocation (6 out of the total of 24

which means that the candidate should allocate a quarter of writing time to this, i.e. about ten minutes).

Candidate's answer

(b) The method used by Gibson in his visual cliff experiment was to see if new-borns had depth perception. The cliff was built with a shallow end and a deep end. Babies were placed at the shallow end while their mothers called them across to the deep end. Ninety-two per cent of the babies refused to cross, which suggests the children had depth perception, but the results remain inconclusive as the babies had six weeks of visual experiences.

Bower's experiment was to find out if babies had size and shape constancy. Through operant conditioning he taught the child to move its head when it saw a cube. Bower drew the conclusion that shape and size constancy is innate. There is a problem with this study, as the children could become bored and look at anything interesting such as cubes. Fantz's study involved seeing what pictures children liked to look at. The pictures ranged from plain to complex and it was timed how long the children looked at the pictures. Fantz concluded that because children looked at the complex picture they had innate perception. He also carried out a similar experiment using a face picture. He found that the children preferred to look at a picture of a face, and so perception is innate. The problem with this study is that again the children could be looking at the most interesting picture.

The nurture studies involved some deprivation studies. Blakemore and Cooper kept kittens in a drum with vertical lines painted inside it. The kittens were allowed out only a few hours a day. When they were released from the drum it was found that they could not see horizontal lines. This suggested that perception is learned. The ethics of this study are to be considered. The long-term effect on the kittens and the psychological stress they encountered at the time have to be understood when assessing this study. Held and Hein carried out another deprivation study, where two kittens were kept in a drum but attached to a carousel. One kitten was active and the other passive. The passive kitten could only move when the active kitten did. When they were let out it was seen that the passive kitten had perceptual deficiencies. This again suggests that perception is learned and also that physical experience is as important as visual experience. The ethics of this study must also be considered, for example the permanent harm to the animals used.

Another method used in the area of perceptual development is cross-cultural studies. Turnbull carried out a study on pygmies. He took them from their home in the dense rainforests to the open plains. Turnbull pointed to a buffalo on the horizon and when the pygmy was asked what it was he replied that it was an ant. This again suggests that perception is learned. Again the methods have to be assessed. Would it be harmful to place a person in a strange environmemt? We should also consider the reliability of cross-cultural studies – observers from Europe may well be biased and not understand the language or practices.

The methods used in the investigation of perceptual development have been deprivation studies and cross-cultural studies, which voice the main issues. Is it necessary to know about kittens' perception, and is that relevant to humans? These studies only show that perception is learned in kittens and not in humans.

Examiner's comment on part (b)

In part (b) the candidate has attempted to discuss three main methods, i.e. work with children, animals, and cross-cultural studies, but the discussion is limited. It appears that the candidate has 'forgotten' the actual question and instead just further described the studies in part (a) and offered some evaluation of the *studies* rather than the *methods*, as required in the question. Inevitably, by describing the studies, one is describing a method, but the lack of direction means that the descriptive component of this part would be given 3 marks out of 6 – the answer is reasonable but limited.

The material offered in terms of an assessment of the methods is not really developed, although some important points are raised though not elaborated. This would be awarded 5 out of 12 marks, again limited, reasonably effective and with some evidence of coherent elaboration.

It could be argued that the candidate had prepared for a nature/nurture essay but that the answer has been adapted to fit the question asked, demonstrating a reasonable level of appropriate knowledge and understanding. The total mark would be 14 out of

24; this is likely to be equivalent to a borderline grade B/C answer at A Level.

Practice essay 2

Describe and evaluate any two theories of pattern recognition in relation to visual perception. (24 marks)

AEB 1997 January

Starting point: This is a 24-mark question with 12 marks for the description of two theories and 12 marks for an evaluation of the same theories.

***Two** theories are required. Candidates discussing only one will receive partial marks (known as partial performance) whereas those who discuss more than two will get the best two credited. It is not a good idea to discuss several theories when two are required because, first, only two will be considered and, second, it wastes valuable time. You could, however, use other theories as a means of evaluation but this must be done explicitly in order to be given credit.*

The following essay was written under examination conditions.

Candidate's answer

Seeing patterns and understanding them is a reductionist phrase. This is due to the complex process it involves. The biological function that the eye performs is that light strikes a series of rods and cones at the back of the retina and is sent along the optic nerve to the thalamus region of the brain via electrical activity. To say this was perception would be incorrect, as this biological effect is sensation and perception begins when the biological function is complete.

One of the first theories of pattern recognition is the Gestalt theory of closure. This theory states that as humans are unhappy perceiving random images of dots, line and colour, we will perceive formations of patterns from the random images. This can be demonstrated when we look at drawn lines on a page. If the lines are evenly spaced we do not perceive a difference, but when the lines are unevenly spaced we perceive them as pairs or shapes. This was described as perceptual organisation and the Gestalt theorists used this to explain pattern recognition.

Another theory was that of perceptual computation put forward by Marr. He described the biological process (sensation) as being instrumental in pattern recognition and not that we were just predisposed to form patterns. Marr explained that patterns are built up from dots, lines and detail and likened this process to how a painting was constructed, the three stages being background (the unfocused area), the block effect (general outline) and the line structure (detail, features, shade, texture, etc.). Marr used the television as an example. The electronic image is constructed from pixels, tiny dots of light varying in colour and shade. When these dots are small enough they are not perceived individually but as a whole image or pattern. For these theories to be fully evaluated, a meaning for patterns must first be established. This is very difficult to specifically define, as patterns are images that are coherent in structure. This can include anything from a simple drawn picture, to trees, to the world in which we live. Both theories can appear reductionist, as pattern recognition is not solely a visual process. Gibson stated that perception is direct and is being constantly updated, but this cannot happen on a purely visual basis as movement and the other senses must be taken into consideration. This can be demonstrated when looking at abstract art; it may appear to represent one thing from a certain angle and represent another when the angle is changed.

All perception is a survival tool and pattern recognition is an integral part of that tool. To recognise patterns is to be aware of your environment and, with all animals, awareness can ensure your survival. Culture as it affects environment can also affect perception; as with Gregory's experiments with paper illusions and African tribes, unfamiliar patterns can fool perception. In the case of the Müller-Lyer lines, because in African culture there were very few carpentered patterns the length of the lines were not in doubt, as they saw the first as drawn lines and did not take perspective into account. This appears to contradict the Gestaltists' theory of closure and suggests that pattern recognition is not standard in all humans but can vary due to cultural differences.

Is pattern recognition an innate ability? Do we all perceive the same? Is seeing really believing? These questions have not been fully explained or described in any one theory. The perception process cannot rely solely on vision and therefore pattern recognition theories are unable to explain the complete process.

Examiner's comment

The candidate has given a reasonably accurate and detailed answer which demonstrated knowledge of the content required in a description of two theories of pattern recognition. The depth of the description of both the Gestalt and Marr theories was slightly limited however, and the range of supporting material lacked detail. The essay was well structured. This part of the question scored 7 marks out of a possible 12.

The evaluation of the theories was slightly less well done. Some appropriate evaluation of the theories was presented, but this tended to be limited and somewhat general in nature. A better answer would have focused directly on the main problems associated with each theory and might have used alternative theories as a means of evaluation. One could also consider applications as a means of positive evaluation as well as empirical studies. The first paragraph served as a general commentary and therefore would gain some credit, though again it was of a general nature. For the evaluative part of this answer, 6 marks were awarded out of a possible 12.

The total was 13 out of a possible 24, likely to be equivalent to a grade C at A level.

KEY RESEARCH SUMMARIES

Article 1

Held, R. and Hein, A. (1963) Movement-produced stimulation in the development of visually guided behaviour, *Journal of Comparative and Physiological Psychology* 56, 607–13.

Background

This study investigates how exposure to the environment affects the development of space perception and an animal's ability to move effectively around the same environment.

The development of normal sensorimotor co-ordination was suspected to depend on normal self-produced movement. In other words, an animal needs to move freely in its environment and to experience feedback from its own movement to develop normally.

Historically, there was considerable interest prior to this study in the role of environmental stimulation in the development of visual perception. It was believed that, in humans, adaptation to distorted worlds (caused by wearing distorting spectacles) was only effective if people were allowed to move around in their new environment. It was observed that hand–eye co-ordination could return to near normal levels with distorted vision if the person was allowed to move their hand *while* watching it move.

Other theorists (Riesen, 1961) argued that just a change in visual stimulation was sufficient for normal visual development. According to this viewpoint the reason why behavioural deficits appeared in animals that were not allowed to move freely around the environment was due to poor unvaried visual stimulation.

Held and Hein designed a study which would investigate the hypothesis that normal visual development was dependent on an animal moving freely in its environment. This study was also designed to challenge Reisen's view of unvaried stimulation by suggesting that behavioural visual deficits can only be avoided by *self-produced* movement in the visual environment.

METHOD

Ten pairs of kittens were used and placed in the apparatus (see Figure 4.3, p. 86). Exactly the same visual stimulation was available to both kittens, but only one kitten controlled its own movement. This meant that only one kitten was actively moving in the environment. The riding or passive kitten received an equivalent amount of visual stimulation as the active kitten but obviously did not control its own movement. The kittens could not see their own paws and bodies, nor could they see each other.

The pairs of kittens were reared in total darkness from birth until they were sufficiently developed to allow one of the pair to move the apparatus and its partner (8–12 weeks). The kittens then had use of the apparatus for three hours a day.

The main tests of visually guided behaviour were:

- *Visually guided paw placement.* Normally reared kittens extend their paws as they are moved slowly towards a table edge, i.e. anticipating contact.
- *The visual cliff test.* See Figure 4.2, p.82.

117

All the active kittens passed the paw placement test but none of the passive kittens did. All the active kittens behaved normally on the visual cliff and would not venture on to the deep side. The passive kittens behaved as if they did not discriminate between the shallow and deep sides.

After 48 hours of freedom in a naturally lit environment the passive kittens behaved normally on both visual tests.

DISCUSSION

The results support the theory that self-produced movement is essential for the development of visually guided behaviour. Visual stimulation is not enough on its own. The authors concluded that visual motor co-ordination develops normally when changes in visual stimulation are brought about by the animal's own movements in its environment.

Article 2

Segall, M.H., Campbell, D.T. and Herskovits, M.J. (1963) Cultural differences in the perception of geometrical illusions, *Science* 139 (22 February), 769–71.

Background

This study was designed to investigate responses to visual illusions of people from different cultural backgrounds. If different responses were made by people from different cultures, this could be taken to support the view that aspects of perception are learned. In other words, as far as perception is concerned it supports the nurture argument (acquired by experience) rather than the nature argument (innate or genetically determined).

Different cultures offer different learning experiences and this should be reflected in the results if perception is influenced by learning.

The authors used the illusions shown in Figure 6.1. Many people tend to think that line (a) is longer in the Müller-Lyer and parallelogram illusion, and that the vertical line is longer than the horizontal line in the other two illusions. They used 39 drawings which were all variations of those in Figure 6.1 and carried out the study over six years, and 1878 participants were used from 17 different groups. These groups consisted of 14 non-European groups in 12 locations in Africa and one in the Philippines. The European groups were (1) a South African group of European descent, (2) American undergraduates, and (3) residents of Illinois.

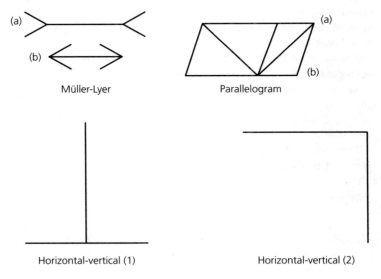

Figure 6.1 **Illusions used by Segall *et al*. (1963)**

The participants had to tell the experimenters which of the two lines of each illusion was the longest. The experimenters also varied the length of the lines in the illusion to try to get an estimate of how much longer the line (normally perceived as shorter) needed to be before both lines appeared the same.

In general the results showed that the three European groups were more likely to be influenced by the Müller-Lyer and parallelogram illusion than the non-European groups.

The non-European groups were more influenced by the horizontal-vertical illusion than the European groups.

However, the authors did find some non-European groups that were even less influenced by the Müller-Lyer and parallelogram illusion than the European groups.

DISCUSSION

The authors interpreted the evidence as support for cultural differences in perception arising because of *learning* how to view things in different environments.

They argued that the European environment is structured with rectangular right-angled objects dominating, and that people see the illusions as corresponding to real three-dimensional images in that environment. Real three-dimensional images have depth and this is inferred from the two-dimensional illusions, making 'nearer' lines seem shorter.

The authors pointed out that the environmental features remain to be identified, but stressed that their findings indicate that there are cultural differences in perception, and these seem to be based on learned factors.

Glossary

The first occurrence of each of these terms is highlighted in **bold** type in the main text.

accommodation (*depth cue*) muscular sensations that occur when the eye brings objects at different distances into focus and which provide information about the distance of the object.

accommodation (*focus*) change in the shape of the lens which is necessary to keep an object in focus on the retina.

affordance Gibson used this concept to imply that the potential use of an object can be perceived directly. For example, we can see that a cup can be used to contain liquid and can be used for drinking, i.e. the cup *affords* drinking.

agnosia a perceptual deficit whereby the person can sense but cannot make sense of one or more features of the environment (see **prosopagnosia**).

albedo the percentage of light reflected from an object.

Ames room distorted room first designed by Adelbert Ames that produces size and distance illusions (see Figure 2.3).

apparent movement the illusion of movement when there isn't any. A typical example is the neon light advertising board that you find at main post offices.

artificial intelligence (AI) the attempt to use computer programs to reproduce human cognitive processes.

astigmatism visual disorder in which the cornea is not perfectly round.

autokinetic effect an illusory effect demonstrated by staring at a stationary point of light in a dark room. After a while the light appears to move around.

autonomic response an automatic response controlled by the autonomic nervous system.

axon the part of the neuron (nerve fibre) which conducts nerve impulses over distances.

binocular cues depth cues that use information from both eyes.

bi-polar cell a neuron which is stimulated by the visual receptors and which sends signals to the retinal ganglion cells.

blind spot an area of the retina that is not sensitive to light because this is where the optic nerve leaves the eye.

bottom-up theories direct perception from sensory information. In other words, perception is directly based on information coming into the sense organs.

cataract clouding of the lens which can be caused by injury or disease.

cones retinal receptor cells that respond to different wavelengths of light used to perceive colour.

constructivist theory theory which proposes that the observer has an internal problem-solving process that transforms the incoming stimulus into a perception.

cornea transparent membrane at the front of the eye.

depth cue information in the environment that helps depth perception such as texture gradient. The environment loses texture definition with distance.

direct perception the idea proposed by J.J. Gibson that we are able to pick up information directly from environmental cues.

distal stimulus the stimulus out in the environment (usually at some distance from the observer).

ecological theory theory based on the study of the relationship between an animal and its environment.

empiricists those who believe that psychological processes are learned.

extrastriate cortex the region around the striate cortex. It receives processed information from the primary visual (striate) cortex.

extrovert a person whose personality is focused on things outside themselves, as opposed to an **introvert**.

familiar size a depth cue. An object's familiar or standard size is used as a source of information in distance perception.

feature detector cells cells in the visual system that respond to particular features in the visual environment (e.g. lines or edges).

figure–ground relationship the ability to perceive an object (the figure) against a background (ground).

flow pattern pattern of visual stimulation that is created when elements in the environment flow past an observer who is moving.

fovea a small area in the retina which contains only cones.

ganglion cells cells in the retina that receive inputs from the bi-polar cells and amacrine cells.

Gestalt School of Psychology A school of psychology that has focused on developing principles of perceptual organisation.

glaucoma a disease of the eye in which increased fluid inside the eye causes too much pressure.

habituation a means of testing infants based on a decrement in attention after repeated visual stimulation.

horizon ratio the proportion of an object which is above the horizon divided by the proportion which is below the horizon.

illusory contour contours are perceived even though they are not physically present in the stimulus.

information processing approach a cognitive approach whereby information is processed in stages by a number of different cognitive systems (e.g. perception, attention, memory, thinking).

introvert see **extrovert**.

kinetic depth effect a phenomenon where an object looks flat when it is stationary but appears to have depth when it moves.

lateral geniculate nucleus (LGN) a relay station to the visual cortex which has a role in processing information.

Law of Pragnanz one of the Gestalt laws of perceptual organisation. It states that, when faced with several alternative perceptions, observers will choose the one that offers the best, simplest and most stable shape.

misapplied size constancy Gregory's principle that visual illusions of size can arise when observers incorrectly apply the mechanisms used for maintaining size constancy in a three-dimensional world to a two-dimensional picture.

monocular cues depth cues that can be used by one eye.

motion parallex a depth cue. Closer objects appear to move faster when viewed by a moving observer than distant objects.

nativists those who believe that psychological processes are innate.

optic array Gibson used this term to refer to the array of information presented to the retina, in other words the pattern of light falling on to the retina which contains all the information needed for direct perception.

optic chiasm the point where the optic nerves cross and send information to both hemispheres of the brain.

optic disc region of the retina where the optic nerve leaves the eye.

optic flow patterns (OFPs) Gibson described how the environment seems to flow past a moving observer and the point to which we are moving stays still.

optic nerve bundle of nerve fibres that carry impulses from the retina to the lateral geniculate nucleus and other structures in the brain.

perception the psychological process of interpretation of sensation, in other words the translation of physical sensory information into a meaningful psychological interpretation of the world.

perceptual constancies a series of phenomena whereby our visual world remains stable. They include size constancy, shape constancy and colour constancy.

perceptual defence for example, when words with a high degree of emotional content are recognised less easily than words of a more neutral nature.

perceptual set a bias or predisposition to perceive aspects of the visual world.

phenomenological approach a philosophical approach whereby information is understood in terms of its immediate experience rather than through an analysis of its physical (scientific) nature.

photoreceptor light receptor cells, i.e. the rods and cones in the retina.

precocial animals which are mobile from birth, as distinct from altricial species.

presbyopia type of far-sightedness caused by hardening of the lens. It occurs with ageing.

prosopagnosia an agnosic condition in which the person can see faces but cannot recognise who the face belongs to.

proximal stimulus process which stimulates the receptors.

retina a complex network of cells which covers the back of the eye.

retinal disparity binocular depth cue which uses the fact that each eye sees a slightly different image of the same scene.

rods light-sensitive cells that respond to light intensity (shades of grey) and is specialised for dim light.

sensation stimulation of the sense organs.

set a bias or predisposition to respond in a particular manner.

stereopsis the ability to discriminate objects in three-dimensional space.

striate cortex (or visual cortex) the visual receiving area of the cortex where the neurons from the LGN terminate.

stroboscopic effect illusion of movement caused by rapid pattern of stimulation on different parts of the retina.

texture gradient a depth cue. The texture of the environment appears to get smoother with distance.

top-down theories cognitive processes construct the world and perception is an active process that makes inferences from sensation.

veridical perception perception which matches the actual physical situation.

visual acuity the capacity to see the fine detail of objects.

visual illusions two-dimensional figures that cause a misperception when viewed (e.g. Müller-Lyer illusion).

References

References

Allport, F.H. (1955) *Theories of Perception and the Concepts of Structure*, New York: John Wiley & Sons.

Aslin, R.N. (1981) Development of smooth pursuit in infants, in D. Fisher, R.A. Monty and J.W. Senders (eds) *Eye Movements: Cognition and Visual Perception*, Hillsdale, NJ: Erlbaum.

—— (1988) Anatomical constraints on oculumotor development: implications for infant perception, in A. Yonas (ed.) *Perceptual Development in Infancy: The Minnesota Symposia on Child Psychology*, Hillsdale, NJ: Lawrence Erlbaum Associates.

Baylis, G.C. and Driver, J. (1995) One-sided edge assignment in vision: figure–ground segmentation and attention to objects, *Current Directions in Psychological Science* 4, 140–6.

Biederman, I. (1987) Recognition-by-components. A theory of human image understanding, *Psychological Review* 94, 115–47.

—— (1990) Higher level vision, in E.N. Osherson, S.M. Kosslyn and J.M. Hollerbach (eds) *An Invitation to Cognitive Science* (Vol. 2), Cambridge, MA: MIT Press.

Blakemore, C. and Cooper, G.G. (1970) Development of the brain depends on the visual environment, *Nature* 228, 477–8.

Bornstein, M.H. (1984) Perceptual development, in M.H. Bornstein and M.E. Lamb (eds) *Developmental Psychology: An Advanced Textbook*, Hillsdale, NJ: Lawrence Erlbaum Associates.

Bornstein, M.H., Krinsky, S.J. and Benasich, A.A. (1986) Fine orientation discrimination and shape constancy in young infants, *Journal of Experimental Child Psychology* 41, 49–60.

Bower, T.G.R. (1966) The visual world of infants, *Scientific American* 215(6), 80–92.

Bruce, C., Desimone, R. and Gross, C.G. (1981) Visual properties of neurons in a polysensory area in the superior temporal sulcus of the macaque, *Journal of Neurophysiology* 46, 369–84.

Bruce, V. and Green, P.R. (1990) *Visual Perception: Physiology, Psychology and Ecology*, 2nd edn, Hove: Lawrence Erlbaum Associates.

Bruner, J.S. and Postman, L. (1949) On the perception of incongruity: a paradigm, *Journal of Personality* 18, 206–23.

Bushnell, I. W. R., Sai, F. and Mullin, J.T. (1989) Neonatal recognition of the mother's face, *British Journal of Developmental Psychology* 7, 3–15.

Campos, J.J., Langer, A. and Krowitz, A. (1970) Cardiac responses on the visual cliff in prelocomotor human infants, *Science* 170, 196–7.

Cave, C.B. and Kosslyn, S.M. (1993) The role of parts and spatial relations in object identification, *Perception* 22, 229–48.

Coren, S. (1981) The interaction between eye movements and visual illusions, in D.F. Fisher, R.A. Monty and J.W. Senders (eds) *Eye Movements: Cognition and Visual Perception*, Hillsdale, NJ: Lawrence Erlbaum Associates.

Coren, S. and Girgus, J.S. (1972) Illusion decrement in intersecting line figures, *Psychnomic Science* 26, 108–10.

—— (1978) *Seeing is Deceiving: The Psychology of Visual Illusions*, Hillsdale, NJ: Lawrence Erlbaum Associates.

Coren, S. and Porac, C. (1983) Subjective contours and apparent depth: A direct test, *Perception and Psychophysics* 33, 197–200.

Coren, S., Porac, C. and Theodor, L.H. (1987) Set and subjective contour, in S. Petry and G.E. Meyer (eds) *The Perception of Illusory Contours*, New York: Springer-Verlag.

Corso, J.F. (1981) *Aging Sensory Systems and Perception*, New York: Praeger.

Day, R.H. (1989) Natural and artificial cues, perceptual compromise and the basis of veridical and illusory perception, in D.Vickers and P.L. Smith (eds) *Human Information Processing: Measures and Mechanisms*, North Holland, The Netherlands: Elsevier Science.

De Lucia, P. and Hochberg, J. (1991) Geometrical illusions in solid objects under ordinary viewing conditions, *Perception and Psychophysics* 50, 547–54.

Deregowski, J. (1972) Pictoral perception and culture. *Scientific American* 227, 82–8.

—— (1980) *Illusions, Patterns and Pictures: A Cross-cultural Perspective*, London: Academic Press.

Duncan, H.F., Gourlay, N. and Hudson, W. (1973) *A Study of Pictorial Representation Among the Bantu and White Primary School Children in South Africa*, Johannesburg: Witwatersrand University Press.

Eysenck, H.J. (1967) *The Biological Basis of Personality*, Springfield, IL: Thomas.

Eysenck, M.W. and Keane, M.T. (1995) *Cognitive Psychology: A Student's Handbook*, 3rd edn, Hove: Lawrence Erlbaum Associates.

Fantz, R.L. (1961) The origin of human form perception, *Scientific American* 204(5), 66–72.

Fantz, R.L. and Yeh, J. (1979) Configural selectivities: critical for development of visual perception and attention, *Canadian Journal of Psychology* 33, 277–87.

Flavell, J.H. (1985) *Cognitive Development*, 2nd edn, Englewood Cliffs, NJ: Prentice-Hall.

Friedman,S.L. and Stevenson, M. (1975) Developmental changes in understanding of implied motion in two-dimensional pictures, *Child Development* 46, 773–8.

Garner, W.R. (1979) Letter discrimination and identification, in A.D. Pick (ed.) *Perception and its Development: A Tribute to Eleanor J. Gibson*, Hillsdale, NJ: Lawrence Erlbaum Associates.

Gibson, E.J. and Walk, R.D. (1960) The visual cliff, *Scientific American* 202(4), 64–71.

Gibson, J.J. (1950) *The Perception of the Visual World*, Boston, MA: Houghton Mifflin.

—— (1986) *The Ecological Approach to Visual Perception*, reprint of 1979 edition, Hillsdale, NJ: Lawrence Erlbaum Associates.

Gliner, J.A., Horvath, S.M. and Mihevic, P.M. (1983) Carbon monoxide and human performance in a single and dual task methodology, *Aviation, Space and Environmental Medicine* 54, 714–17.

Goldstein, E.B. (1999) *Sensation and Perception*, 5th edn, Pacific Grove: Brooks/Cole Publishing Co.

Goren, C.C., Sarty, M. and Wu, P.Y.K. (1975) Visual following and pattern discrimination of face-like stimuli by newborn infants, *Pediatrics* 56, 544–9.

Gregor, A.J. and McPherson, D. (1965) A study of susceptibility to geometrical illusions among cultural outgroups of Australian aborigines, *Psychologiia, Africana* 11, 490–9.

Gregory, R.L. (1990) *Eye and Brain: The Psychology of Seeing*, 4th edn, London: Weidenfeld & Nicolson.

—— (1996) Twenty-five years after 'The Intelligent Eye', *The Psychologist* 9, 452–3.

Gregory, R.L. and Wallace, J. (1963) *Recovery from Early Blindness*, Cambridge: Heffer.

Hagen, M. and Jones, R. (1978) Cultural effects on pictorial perception: how many words is one picture really worth?, in R.Walk and H. Pick (eds) *Perception and Experience*, New York: Plenum.

Haith, M.M. (1980) *Rules that Babies Look By*, Hillsdale, NJ: Lawrence Erlbaum Associates.

Halpern, D.F. (1986) *Sex Differences in Cognitive Abilities*, Hillsdale, NJ: Lawrence Erlbaum Associates.

Harkins, S. and Green, R.G. (1975) Discriminability and criterion differences between extroverts and introverts during vigilance. *Journal of Research in Personality* 9, 335–40.

Harris, C.S. (1980) Insight or out of sight? Two examples of perceptual plasticity in the human adult, in C.S. Harris (ed.) *Visual Coding and Adaptability*, Hillsdale, NJ: Lawrence Erlbaum Associates.

Hartman, A. and Hollister, L. (1963) Effect of mescaline, lysergic acid diethylamide and psilocybin on colour perception, *Psychopharmacologia* 4, 441–5.

Haskins, R. and McKinney, J.D. (1976) Relative effects of response tempo and accuracy on problem solving and academic achievement, *Child Development* 47, 690–6.

Held, R. and Bossom, J. (1961) Neonatal deprivation and adult rearrangement: complementary techniques for analysing plastic sensory–motor co-ordinations, *Journal of Comparative and Physiological Psychology* 54, 33–7.

Held, R. and Hein, A. (1963) Movement-produced stimulation in the devlopment of visually guided behaviour, *Journal of Comparative and Physiological Psychology* 56, 872–6.

Hershenson, M., Munsinger, H. and Kessen, W. (1965) Preference for shapes of intermediate variability in the newborn human, *Science* 147, 630–1.

Hess, E.H. (1950) Development of the chick's response to light and shade cues of depth. *Journal of Comparative and Physiological Psychology*, 43, 112–22.

Hochberg, J. (1971) Perception: 11. Space and movement, in J.W. Kling and L.A. Riggs (eds) *Woodworth and Schlosberg's Experimental Psychology*, New York: Holt, Rinehart and Winston.

Hochberg, J. and Brooks, V. (1962) Pictorial recognition as an unlearned ability. A study of one child's performance, *American Journal of Psychology* 75, 624–8.

Hoffer, A. and Osmond, H. (1967) *The Hallucinogens*, New York: Academic Press.

Hubel, D.H. (1977) Functional architecture of macaque monkey visual cortex, *Proceedings of the Royal Society of London, Series B* 198, 1–59.

Hubel, D.H. and Wiesel, T.N. (1959) Receptive fieldings of single neurons in the cat's cortex, *Journal of Physiology* 160, 106–54.

Hudson, W. (1960) Pictorial depth perception in subcultural groups in Africa, *Journal of Social Psychology* 52, 183–208.

Hurvich, L.M. (1981) *Color Vision*, Sunderland, MA: Sinauer Associates.

Ittelson, W.H. (1952) *The Ames Demonstration in Perception*, New York: Hafner.

Jahoda, G. (1966) Geometric illusions and environment: a study in Ghana, *British Journal of Psychology* 57, 193–9.

Johannson, G. (1975) Visual motion perception, *Scientific American* 232, 76–89.

Kagan, J. (1971) *Change and Continuity in Infancy*, New York: John Wiley & Sons.

Kagan, J., Lapidus, D.R. and Moore, N. (1978) Infant antecedants of cognitive functioning: a longitudinal study, *Child Development* 49, 1005–23.

Kohler, I. (1962) Experiments with goggles, *Scientific American* 206, 62–86.

Kuchuk, A., Vibbert, M. and Bornstein, M.H. (1986) The perception of smiling and its experiential correlates in 3-month old infants, *Child Development* 57, 1054–61.

Lee, D.N. and Lishman, J.R. (1975) Visual proprioceptive control of stance, *Journal of Human Movement Studies* 1, 87–95.

Levy, D.L., Lipton, R.B. and Holzman, P.S. (1981) Smooth pursuit eye movements: effects of alcohol and chloral hydrate, *Journal of Psychiatric Research* 16, 1–11.

Logothetis, N.K. and Pauls, J. (1995) Psychological and physiological evidence for viewer-centred object representation in the primate, *Cerebral Cortex* 5, 270–88.

Luria, A.R. (1973) *The Working Brain*, London: Penguin.

McGinnies, E. (1949) Emotionality and perceptual defence, *Psychological Review* 56, 244–51.

McGuinness, D. (1976) Sex differences in the organisation of perception and cognition, in B. Lloyd and U. Archer (eds) *Exploring Sex Differences*, New York: Academic Press.

McKenzie, B.E., Tootell, H.E. and Day, R.H. (1980) Development of visual size constancy during the first year of human infancy, *Developmental Psychology* 16, 163–74.

Marr, D. (1982) *Vision: A Computational Investigation into the Human Representation and Processing of Visual Information*, San Francisco: W.H. Freeman.

Marr, D. and Hildreth, E. (1980) Theory of edge detection, *Proceedings of the Royal Society of London B* 207, 187–217.

Marr, D. and Nishihara, H.K. (1978) Representation and recognition of the spatial organisation of three-dimensional, *Proceedings of the Royal Society of London B* 200, 269–94.

Matlin, M.W. and Foley, H.J. (1992) *Sensation and Perception*, 3rd edn, Boston, MA: Allyn & Bacon.

Meyer, G.E. and Petry, S. (1987) Top-down and bottom-up: the illusory contour as a microcosm of issues in perception, in S. Petry and G.E. Meyer (eds) *The Perception of Illusory Contours*, New York: Springer-Verlag.

Miller, R.J., Pigion, R.G. and Martin, K.D. (1985) The effects of ingested alcohol on accommodation, *Perception and Psychophysics* 37, 407–14.

Navon, D. (1977) Forest before trees: the precedence of global features in visual perception, *Cognitive Psychology* 9, 353–83.

Neisser, U. (1976) *Cognition and Reality*, San Francisco: Freeman.

Nelson, C.A. and Horowitz, F.D. (1987) Visual motion perception in infancy: a review and synthesis, in P.Salapatek and L. Cohen (eds) *Handbook of Infant Perception* (Vol. 2), New York: Academic Press.

Palmer, S.E. (1975) The effects of contextual scenes on the identification of objects, *Memory and Cognition* 3, 519–26.

Parlee, M.B. (1983) Menstrual rhythms in sensory processes: a review of fluctuations in vision, olfaction, audition, taste and touch, *Psychological Bulletin* 93, 539–48.

Pascalis, O., de Schoenen, S., Morton, J., Deruelle, C. and Fabre-Grenet, M. (1995) Mother's face recognition by neonates: a replication and an extension, *Infant Behaviour and Development* 18, 79–85.

Pedersen, D.M. and Wheeler, J. (1983) The Müller-Lyer illusion among Navajos, *Journal of Social Psychology* 121, 3–6.

Pick, H.L. (1987) Information and the effects of early perceptual experience, in N. Eisenberg (ed.) *Contemporary Topics in Developmental Psychology*, New York: John Wiley & Sons.

Pomerantz, J.R. and Lockhead, G.R. (1991) Perception of structure: an overview, in G.R.Lockhead and J.R. Pomerantz (eds) *Perception of Structure*, Washington, DC: American Psychological Association.

Ramachandran, V.S. and Anstis, S.M. (1986) The perception of apparent motion, *Scientific American* (May), 102–9.

Regan, D. and Beverley, K.I. (1984) Figure–ground segregation by motion contrast and by luminance contrast, *Journal of the Optical Society of America* A, 433–42.

Rhee, K., Kim, D and Kim,Y. (1965) The effects of smoking on night vision *14th Pacific Medical Conference*.

Riesen, A.H. (1947) The development of visual perception in man and chimpanzee, *Science* 106, 107–8.

—— (1961) Studying perceptual development using the technique of sensory deprivation, *Journal of Nervous and Mental Diseases* 132, 21–5.

—— (1965) Effects of early deprivation of photic stimulation, in S. Oster and R. Cook (eds) *The Biosocial Bases of Mental Retardation*, Baltimore, MD: Johns Hopkins University Press.

Rock, I. (1983) *The Logic of Perception*, Cambridge, MA: MIT Press.

Rock, I. (1986) Cognitive intervention in perceptual processing, in T.J. Knapp and L.C. Robertson (eds) *Approaches to Cognition: Contrasts and Controversies*, Hillsdale, NJ: Lawrence Erlbaum Associates.

Segall, M.H., Campbell, D.T. and Herskovits, M.J. (1963) Cultural differences in the perception of geometrical illusions, *Science* 139, 769–71.

Selfridge, O.G. (1959) 'Pandemonium: a paradigm for learning', in *Symposium on the Mechanisation of Thought Processes*, London: HMSO.

Sheedy, J.E., Bailey, I.L., Buri, M. and Bass, E. (1986) Binocular vs. monocular task performance, *American Journal of Optometry and Physiological Optics* 63, 839–46.

Shiffar, M. and Freyd, J.J. (1993) Timing and apparent motion path choice with human body photographs, *Psychological Science* 4, 379–84.

Stratton, G.M. (1896) Some preliminary experiments on vision without inversion of the retinal image, *Psychological Review* 3, 611–17.

Tart, C. (1971) *On Being Stoned*, Palo Alto: Science and Behaviour Books.

Thouless, R.H. (1931) Phenomenal regression to the real object, *British Journal of Psychology* 21, 339–59.

Toch, H.H. and Schulte, R. (1961) Readiness to perceive violence as a result of police training, *British Journal of Psychology* 52, 389–93.

Tovee, M.J., Rolls, E.T. and Azzopardi, P. (1994) Translation invariance in the response to faces of single neurons in the temporal visual cortex areas of the alert macaque, *Journal of Neurophysiology* 72, 1049–60.

Von Senden, M. (1960) *Space and Sight: The Perception of Space and Shape in the Congenitally Blind Before and After Operations*, trans. P. Heath, London: Methuen (originally published 1932).

Wallach, H. (1948). Brightness constancy and the nature of achromatic colours, *Journal of Experimental Psychology* 38, 310–24.

Walton, G.E., Bower, N.J.A. and Power, T.G.R. (1992) Recognition of familiar faces by newborns, *Infant Behaviour and Development* 15, 265–9.

Ward, T.B. (1985) Individual differences in processing stimulus dimensions: relation to selective processing ability, *Perception and Psychophysics* 37, 471–82.

Watt, R.J. and Morgan, M.J. (1984) Spatial filters and the localisation of luminance changes in human vision, *Vision Research* 24, 1387–97.

Weale, R.A. (1986) Aging and vision, *Vision Research* 26, 1507–12.

Weiskrantz, L. (1956) Behavioural changes associated with ablation of the amygdaloid complex in monkeys, *Journal of Comparative and Physiological Psychology* 49, 381–91.

Weisstein, N. and Wong, E. (1986) Figure-ground organization and the spatial and temporal responses of the visual system, in E.C. Schwab and H.C. Nusbaum (eds) *Pattern Recognition by Humans and Machines (Vol. 2)*, New York: Academic Press.

Wertheimer, M. (1912) Experimentelle Studien uber das Sehen von Bewegung, *Zeitschrift fur Psychologie* 61, 161–265.

Witkin, H.A., Dyk, R.B., Faterson, H.F., Goodenough, D.R. and Karp, S.A. (1962) *Psychological Differentiation*, New York: John Wiley & Sons.

Index